RITA WARREN was born in Italy in the Mussolini era, and came to America as the bride of a U.S. staff sergeant. As a mother of three living in Brockton, Massachusetts, Rita Warren one day in 1969 heard her 12-year-old daughter Teresa comment: "Mom, they won't let us pray." The remark spurred Rita Warren to launch a legal battle which would ultimately affect the whole country.

DICK SCHNEIDER, Contributing Editor of *Guideposts* magazine, has contributed numerous articles to national publications and co-authored *Road Block to Moscow* with Nick Savoca and *I Dared to Call Him Father* with Bilquis Sheikh.

"Two hundred years from now, I trust that Americans will be able to thank people like Rita Warren who fight within our system, sustained by a deep faith in God, for liberty and truth."

John McCormack, former speaker of the U.S. House of Representatives

". . . extremely interesting, and carries a very potent and needed message."

Norman Vincent Peale

Rita Warren /with Dick Schneider

mom, they won't let us pray...

√ a chosen book

Key-Word Edition
PUBLISHED BY WORD BOOKS, PUBLISHER
WACO, TEXAS

Scripture references in this volume, unless otherwise identified, are from the King James Version of the Bible.

Scripture quotations identified RSV are from the Revised Standard Version of the Bible, copyrighted 1946, 1952, © 1971 and 1973 by the Division of Christian Education of the National Council of Churches, and are used by permission.

Library of Congress Cataloging in Publication Data

Warren, Rita.
    Mom, they won't let us pray . . .

    1. Religion in public schools—Brockton, Mass. 2. Religion in public schools—United States. 3. Warren, Rita. I. Schneider, Dick, joint author. II. Title.
LC113.B76W37   337'.1   75–25629
ISBN 0-8499-4110-5

MOM, THEY WON'T LET US PRAY . . .

A Chosen Book
Published by Word Books, Publisher
First Key-Word edition 1978

Printed in the United States of America

TO all the children in America.
May they always have the freedom
to pray wherever they wish.

My deepest gratitude to all the news media who have helped in this battle. May they continue their good work until the war is won and God's will is fulfilled.

Contents

Foreword

Rita Warren, an Italian immigrant with a fifth-grade education, of limited means, again demonstrates the effectiveness of the American democracy. Working through lawful legislative processes, she was, in my opinion, the most important single person behind the movement to return prayer to the public schools of Massachusetts. It proves all over again the forcefulness of a system that—nearing its bicentennial—still works, still demonstrates that the common man has his chance to say.

The real power behind Mrs. Warren's effectiveness is, of course, her faith in God. Hers is a faith that has been tested many times, through the rigors of her childhood years during World War II in Naples, and through rearing a family which includes a crippled, retarded child. However, with steadfast faith in the power of Jesus Christ, she has forged ahead in complete assurance that whenever one asks God, believing, He will answer.

"Faith moves mountains," says Mrs. Warren, and during the years that I have known her, I have watched her faith move many mountains.

Mrs. Warren believes in the love as preached by our Lord and Saviour, Jesus Christ, and professes no hate toward any of her adversaries. Reflecting this is her relationship with Madalyn Murray O'Hair, the Atheist, who is probably her most outstanding opponent in the prayer issue. Yet, the two meet in an atmosphere of mutual respect. They argue issues without rancor or hate. "Through God" says Rita Warren of Madalyn O'Hair, "I love her very much."

True, Rita Warren is an immigrant. But like so many of those who have come before her, she has demonstrated the true meaning of American citizenship: involvement, interest, and a pledging of oneself to the pursuit of high ideals. In doing so, she has given up comfort, relaxation, and security.

Two hundred years from now, I trust that Americans will be able to thank people like Rita Warren who fight within our system—sustained by a deep faith in God— for liberty and truth.

> JOHN W. McCORMACK
> Former Speaker of the
> House of Representatives and
> Congressman from Massachusetts

1.

"Mom, They Won't Let Us Pray..."

It was Autumn in New England. The maples along Court street in our little community of Brockton had caught fire with the frost. And on that bright October day in 1969, as I pushed the vacuum across our living-room rug, the orange and gold flashed through the windows and I thanked the Lord for His beauty, for this little house, for a rug to vacuum.

I thought back through the years since I first came to this country. So much had happened, good things and bad things. And above all I had so much to be thankful for. My son Bobby now grown and married, who lived in New Hampshire; Anita, my retarded nineteen-year-old daughter, who sat in her bedroom watching television; and Teresa, my twelve-year-old. And I was thankful for the husband I once had.

I glanced at the clock. It would soon be time for Teresa to be home. She had been attending our parochial school. It had closed and just a few days ago she had transferred to the Brockton Junior-High. I wondered how she liked it.

I moved a chair to vacuum under it and flinched at the threadbare portion of the carpet I was trying to hide. *How many more years could we make it last?* I wondered. Just then Teresa came in the door. I glanced at her as she came into the room. She had her father's height and dark good looks, and appeared much older than her twelve years.

11

"How was it today?" I asked, continuing to push the vacuum.

Teresa sank down on the couch, tossed her long, dark hair away from her eyes, and said: "Mom, do you know that they won't let us pray in school?"

"You're kidding," I laughed incredulously, and switched off the vacuum. "Who said so?"

"A teacher, Mom."

I sat down on the couch next to her.

"A teacher? What happened?"

"Well, after I'd been there a few days, I noticed there was something very different from my other school. There was never any time for prayer, even at the start of the day. When I asked a teacher if we ever prayed, she said of course not, because it was unconstitutional."

"You mean it's against the law?" I asked.

"I guess so," said Teresa, scruffling the ears of Lupo, our dog who had come in to greet her. "The teacher said an Atheist took the prayer out of school."

"An Atheist? What's an Atheist?"

"Someone who doesn't believe in God," said Teresa.

"You've got to be kidding!" I exclaimed. I didn't know there even was such a person.

"Well, anyway, it all sounds pretty stupid to me," said Teresa as she got up and walked into the kitchen.

An Atheist, I wondered to myself. And then something jogged my memory. I sank back into the couch. A vague recollection about some kind of a court decision years ago came back to me—something about a woman who took prayer out of school. The legal arguments were 'way beyond me.

But now I was deeply concerned. A court rule to take prayer out of the public school? I felt they might as well take God out of the school. With Him gone, what would follow? A further slackening in moral standards, which seemed to be going downhill anyway these past several years?

And now, my daughter had been told right out by a teacher that she couldn't pray in school!

A foreboding sense of oppression came over me that stirred dark memories from my youth. I shuddered as I thought of those terrible days in Italy where I had grown up during World War II. Under the rule of an iron fist, I remembered being told what I could think, and what I could not think. Freedom came when I emigrated to the United States as an eighteen-year-old war bride. My great joy was becoming a citizen of a country where everyone was free to think and speak as he pleased.

I sat staring out the window into the blazing red and gold of a giant maple. This was the country, wasn't it, where all religions were tolerated—where everyone was free to worship God as his heart directed?

And yet, my child was now forbidden to pray in her school. But still, it was a law. And we must obey the law.

"Teresa," I called. She walked in from the kitchen, a glass of milk in one hand, a cookie in the other.

"Sit down, hon." As best I could, I told Teresa what little I knew about the court decision. "I don't know much about this situation. But I'll try to find out."

Teresa sat pensively for a moment, swallowed the rest of her milk from the glass, then jumped up and gathered her books. "Well, I still don't understand it, Mom. But right now I've got to get at this math homework."

She went into her room and I peeked in her door later. Instead of doing her homework, she was sitting quietly at her desk with a faraway look in her eyes.

I continued my vacuuming and a little later Teresa came back into the living room.

"Mom," she said, "I've got a question."

I turned off the vacuum; it looked like I'd never get the rug done today. There was something unusual about the way Teresa looked at me.

"I was thinking, Mom," she said, "that if it's possible for one person who doesn't believe in God to take prayer out of school, why can't someone like you who has so much faith in God put it back in?"

I shook my head and smiled.

"But you always said," Teresa continued, "that with God all things are possible."

I stood looking into her dark brown eyes, and put my hand on her shoulder.

"Yes, Teresa, that is true. And I still believe it." I thought of her sister, Anita, who now sat in the bedroom watching television. Anita was born so deformed and retarded that doctors had given her little chance to live. I could never count the hours I spent on my knees praying for her. And the Lord had surely answered.

Yet, praying for my own child was one thing, I thought. *Changing a government law was another.* I chuckled to myself. Who was I, a forty-one-year-old Italian immigrant woman with only a fifth-grade education to fight a court decision of the United States of America? Life was difficult enough as a mother alone. I smiled at Teresa and shook my head. "Honey, you get the water ready for the macaroni while I finish this vacuuming."

As the three of us sat down to our pasta that night, we bowed our heads and Anita, her long black hair falling about her misshapen little face, clasped her clubbed hands before her and said her grace. "God is great . . . God is good . . . let us thank Him . . . for . . . our food. *Amen.*" Each word was a struggle for her to form. Yet each syllable, strained as it was, was a testimony of God's power. For this was the child who, according to medical specialists, had no hope of living, much less of speaking or comprehending anything.

Supper was very quiet. And as we washed the dishes, Teresa still said little, unlike her usual exuberant self as she'd tell about her friends and teachers. I knew what was on her mind. Yet, I could not give an answer to this child who I had taught to depend on our Lord for everything. Her first words in the morning and her last at night were spoken in prayer. She had learned to trust Him completely and He had never failed her.

Nor had He failed me, for that matter. Because of Him we had this little gray house in suburban Boston. Through Him we always had food on the table. In every way He had provided for us.

After supper, the girls went to their rooms and I sat down in the living room and tried to read the evening paper. I do not remember what I read that evening. But I will never forget two things that happened to me that night: I had an unusual dream, and later I became violently ill. At the time these seemed to be two entirely unrelated events. It wasn't until some time later that I saw them as part of God's chain of events.

I am certainly not a mystic—but that dream was not an ordinary one. It still burns in my mind as vividly as it did the night it took place. And though it had that unearthly, unreal quality of so many dreams, it still is one of the most real things that has ever happened to me.

At eleven o'clock that night I decided to go to bed. By then I had convinced myself that I wouldn't have to think about Teresa's question any more. Besides, I told myself, when she got a little older she would understand that there is a limit to what one person can do. Laws, court decisions, and government affairs were so complex.

I crawled into bed, said my prayers, and then lay there. I could hear the evening breeze rustling the maple leaves outside. Gradually, the leafy whisper faded in with the rhythmic breathing of my two daughters. In some ways I was glad that our house was such a little cracker box in that such sounds could travel through the walls. They were comforting. And then, again, I saw Teresa asking me that question: If one woman who doesn't believe in God can get prayer taken out of school, why can't someone who does have faith put it back in?

As naturally as if I were talking to a friend, the idea popped into my mind as if from the Lord Himself: "Have you really listened to Teresa's question?"

"O Lord," I breathed, "what could a little ignorant person like me do?"

"Don't forget," came the answer. "I like to work through the weak, the little people, the ones the world calls foolish."

And then I muttered the handful of words that sounded so easy at the time, "All right, Lord," I said. "If You really want me to do something, I will obey. But You must show me the way. . . ."

An automobile horn sounded on the street and I came to with a start. *Oh! Was I thinking or dreaming? What had I just said?* I thought. *Imagine!* I laughed. I closed my eyes again, turned off such silly ideas, released my thoughts to Him, and relaxed under the sheets.

The dream was unlike any that I had ever had before. I found myself walking down a broad street toward Saint Coleman's Church in our old neighborhood. Suddenly, something began to take place in the sky. I looked up, and in my dream I saw a pair of hands materialize; they almost covered the sky. Then slowly the hands began to open. In awe, I saw the sky brighten and in the radiance appeared the face of Jesus. He looked at me, His face gentle. And then I heard Him say: "They shall do to you what they have done unto Me." I stepped back awestruck. *Could I really be hearing Him right? Was I to be crucified?* It wasn't that I feared this. It was just that I felt that I was not worthy even to suffer as He did. (There just wasn't any way for me to know at this time that, in fact, I *was* to be persecuted, jailed, and vilified.)

Then the golden radiance faded. And I felt as if I

were falling free through the air, down . . . down
. . . down. Suddenly I struck the ground. Black-robed
priests from the church ran up to me. One leaned over
me saying, "Rita, get up. I will help you. Rita, get up."

And there I was in my bedroom again, the morning
light streaming through the window. Teresa was standing at the door of my room calling, "Mom, get up; I
have to get to school."

And then occurred the second of the two strange
events of that remarkable day. For as I started to rise,
I fell back on the bed gasping in pain. Something was
stabbing me in the right side. As I lay there struggling
for breath, the pain increased. I couldn't breathe. Then
my entire body started becoming numb as one's jaw
does when the dentist shoots it full of Novocain. I
could hardly keep from screaming.

"Teresa . . . honey," I gasped. "Please call an
ambulance. I must get to the hospital."

Her face whitened. "Oh, Mommy," she said, looking
at me in terror.

"Honey," I pleaded, "please call. . . ."

She turned and ran to the phone.

Within minutes two white-coated ambulance men
entered my room with a stretcher. As they carried me
through the hall, I could hear Teresa explaining to
Anita that I had to go away for a while but would be
home soon.

My heart cried out, "God, please help my girls!"

Gently, they lifted me into the back of the ambulance. One attendant sat by me taking my pulse. I
looked up at him. "I know . . ." I murmured, "I know
I'm going to die."

As we raced through the leaf-filled streets of Boston,
siren wailing, I could see flashes of October blue and
gold through the windows. I had gasped out the name
of New England Baptist Hospital, where my doctor was
on the staff.

Finally, he was examining me in the hospital. As he

probed and prodded, my breathing became increasingly more difficult, and I still couldn't feel my body. Between gasps, I asked my doctor to call Father McCormick. I trusted this man, for he had been like a father to my daughters. In my dream he was the one who offered to help.

Soon his genial Irish face was at the door of my room. I was still in pain in spite of the drugs they were now giving me. He bent over me. "Rita, what happened?"

"Father," I said, "I have already confessed my sins to my Heavenly Father. I called to ask you for something. If I die, please help my girls, especially Anita. Promise that you will never let them put her into a state institution."

He nodded, his quiet, blue eyes full of compassion.

"But, Father," I continued, "if I live, I feel that I now have something very important to do for God."

He leaned forward toward me from his chair. "What is it, Rita? You know that I'll try to help you."

I almost sat up in bed. "Father," I said, "I had the strangest dream last night."

He listened intently as I described my dream. When I was through I found myself saying the words that were to affect my life so directly for years to come. The words came to my lips easily for the message had been burned into my heart last night when Teresa challenged me.

"Father, we must make it possible for children to pray again in their public schools."

He looked at me strangely. "Rita," he said, shaking his head and smiling sadly, "I'm afraid *that* is impossible."

Already I was beginning to hear faint echoes of the Lord's words: "It won't be easy, Rita."

Despite my pain, I turned my head and fixed my eyes on the priest. "Father, with God everything is possible."

"Rita," he patted my forehead. "You are not yourself now. Let us talk about this again when you are well."

I half raised myself on my elbow. I could not let him leave without making some acknowledgment of my dream. It seemed important that someone else on earth recognize it with me—to make a commitment to it.

"Father," I gasped, "promise me on the Bible that when prayer does come back to all the schools in America, you will ring the bells at Saint Coleman's."

He saw the anguished plea in my eyes, leaned over, and said: "Heavenly Father, as a man and a priest, I promise you that if this happens I will ring the bells at Saint Coleman's, and declare that Jesus Christ has put prayer back in school." He gently placed his hand on my head, quietly blessed me, and left the room.

Settled back in bed and alone once more, I began to wonder about my dream. Was I being presumptuous to think it was a message from the Lord? Or was it just a dream and nothing else? As I lay there studying the cracks in the ceiling plaster, my mind drifted back through the years. I began to think of all the other dreams in which I had placed my trust, dreams which like the wandering cracks in the ceiling led nowhere.

2.

Duce! Duce! Duce!

Ala sinistra, ala destra! Ala sinistra, ala destra! Left, right! Left, right! The Naples sun tanned my nine-year-old arms as I marched up the *Via Amadeo* with five hundred other girls of the *Piccole Italiane,* the youth corps. Today was a momentous occasion for Naples. For *Il Duce* had come to our city to make an important speech. As we marched, our white gloves swinging smartly, I was careful not to let my newly whitened shoes brush against my knee socks. Mama had spent hours preparing my uniform, pressing the pleats on my black gabardine skirt, ironing my white piqué blouse, black tie, and brushing the black felt beret. On my blouse I proudly wore the Fascist insignia, the rods and axe bound together with thongs, the ancient symbol of authority of the Roman Empire, the empire that was now alive again under our great leader, Benito Mussolini.

Il Duce visited many major cities in Italy. And everyone loved him for it. Now this was Naples' opportunity to show our love, loyalty, and appreciation for what he had done for us. Il Duce, the rescuer of our country, the savior of our people!

I had heard this said many times, especially by my favorite uncle. Uncle Lorenzo was a tall, handsome man who had fought in World War I. When recalling earlier days, his dark eyes would alight and he'd reach into his closet and lovingly bring out the black shirt he wore when he marched on Rome for Mussolini.

"Ah!" he would exclaim, "without us war veterans and Il Duce there would be no Italy today." He told of dark days following the Great War, of unemployment, hunger, men on strike, and fighting in the streets.

"The Communists were about to take over," Uncle Lorenzo would mutter. "But Il Duce knew what to do," he continued, tapping his head wisely. He told how Mussolini got himself elected to parliament in 1921.

"And then in 1922," Uncle Lorenzo warmed to his story, "under the *Fasci di combattimento,* we organized. And we marched! Yes, we marched right into Rome!" Now Uncle Lorenzo would struggle into his black shirt and begin to march around the room. "And," he continued, his dark eyes flashing, "old King Victor Emmanuel let us into Rome. Then he called on Il Duce who was waiting in Milan to come there and form his cabinet.

"And *that,*" he laughed, slapping his thigh, "is how we soldiers and our leader saved our country!"

I hung onto his every word for Uncle Lorenzo made my history book come alive. Of all my school subjects, history was my favorite. When Mama would visit school, my teacher would point to me. "Mathematics? Science? Language? Nothing," he would say, shaking his head. "But history? *Magnifico!* She remembers *everything!"*

I was fascinated by how governments developed, and how they worked from the days of the Caesars to the present. I remembered Mama telling me how, in 1928, the Italian parliamentary government had become the Fascist government. Her explanation didn't sound quite like my school book but Mama muttered that was because we children were only allowed to read *one* history book in school these days. Some things Mama said Il Duce did didn't quite sound democratic but, then, he seemed to be serving our country well. And he seemed to be everywhere. My early readers carried such phrases as, "The eyes of the Duce are on every one of you." Then I'd look up and there on the wall would be his picture looking down on me. MUSSOLINI IS ALWAYS RIGHT, said the words under the picture.

"He *is* right," said Uncle Lorenzo who talked about marshes being drained, about new *autostrade* connecting our cities, and jobs for everyone.

"Ah," he would say dreamily, "because of him we are a great nation again."

Today, however, as I marched up *Via Amadeo* it would be Uncle Lorenzo whom I would particularly thank. Because of his connection with the government, I, Rita Settembre, would be honored above all girls in Naples. For I would have the distinction of presenting the official bouquet from Naples to our leader.

Ala sinistra, ala destra! Ala sinistra, ala destra! Now our marching group swung column right down the street leading to the piazza. It was near my father's business. My father was a glove manufacturer. I would often prowl around the huge stone building which was his factory and watch the workers magically transform the supple Neapolitan leather into beautiful gloves. My father's business did well.

Was it because of our leader that things were going so well? It seemed to be a wonderful time to be a child in Italy, especially to be one of the Settembres. We were a large and prosperous family. Besides me, Mama and Papa had my sister Enza, and my two brothers, Raphael and Federico. At age nine I was the baby of the family.

Ala sinistra, ala destra! Ala sinistra, ala destra! Most of our family believed in Il Duce, it seemed to me, almost in the same way we believed in God. Mussolini taught us faith. Faith in strength! Faith in the present! Faith in marching men and rolling tanks. Power would keep us safe and prosperous. *Ala sinistra, ala destra!*

Ala sinistra, ala destra! Our squadron flowed from the cool shade of the narrow street into the crowded sunlit piazza.

And there it was: the platform from which Il Duce would address us. The crowd flowed around it like the tide around a rock. We marched into an open area which had been roped off and came to parade rest, maintaining our formation. I looked back and saw black felt berets stretching as far as I could see. And behind them the people with eager expectant faces.

And then he arrived in a flurry of motorcycles and big black limousines. The crowd exploded into applause, the band broke into the Fascist anthem *"Giovinezza,"* and Il Duce strode up the steps of the platform. I had never seen anyone so handsome. Standing resplendent in his beautifully tailored tan and black uniform, his head held back, his jaw outthrust, he was a living statue of strength.

Uncle Lorenzo walked up behind me carrying a huge bouquet of flowers. He placed them in my arms, then pushed me in the back hissing, *"Avanti! Avanti!"*

I seemed to be floating as I moved toward the platform. I could not even feel my legs move as I ascended the steps, holding the flowers out before me. As I approached him, Il Duce's broad, sun-tanned face smiled down at me.

Now I was close enough to see the medals on his huge chest; they sparkled and glistened in the sun.

I thrust the bouquet toward him, feeling like a maiden making a votive offering in the old Roman temples we had read about in school.

"Grazie," he said, his voice low. Then he leaned forward, lowering his massive head until the tassel on his hat fell forward as he presented his cheek to be kissed. I stretched on tiptoe as I leaned into that broad jaw. The stubble pricked my lips as I pressed them against what seemed to be a wall of granite.

Then, flushed with a strange mixture of pride and

embarrassment, I stepped back, offered the Fascist salute, my right arm and hand held straight up, quickly turned, and made my way down the steps. I was in a daze. All I knew was that the crowd was roaring like ocean waves breaking on a rocky shore: *"Duce! Duce! Duce!"*

Breathless, I stopped at the bottom of the steps. Uncle Lorenzo, his face beaming with pride, took my hand and led me back to my place in the formation.

Then Il Duce started his speech, his strong, musical voice booming from the loudspeakers across the crowded piazza.

Now, as we settled ourselves for a long wait, my heart began to resume its normal beat. From experience we knew how long Il Duce could speak. We marveled at how long he could continue speaking without having anything from which to read. So while babies squirmed in their mothers' arms and little boys shifted from one foot to another, everyone stood listening attentively.

Il Duce's voice boomed on as the sun slowly moved over the piazza. My bouquet, lying on the table next to him, had begun to wither and my eyes burned. I looked past the speaker's stand into the hazy horizon, resting my eyes on Mount Vesuvius, now a soft blue pyramid in the late afternoon sun.

Now Il Duce's voice rose and I caught the words *United States*. My heart caught. My brother, Raphael, had been born there. My family had lived there several years before returning to Italy where I was born. But here in the hot sun of the piazza that seemed so far away. Besides, my faith was in this savior speaking before us; he would never let any of us down. And then, insistently in my memory came the voice of Mama: "Remember, Rita, he is just a man, not God."

His voice thundered on and then his words rang out on the afternoon air with the promise that the new Roman empire "shall last forever!"

Something icy clutched my heart. I looked up again

at the blue slope of Vesuvius and my eyes traveled down its side to where I knew lay the cold, gray ashes of Pompeii, the city which its builders expected to last forever. I felt chilled and shuddered from a nameless fear.

Seasons passed. By 1939, our ally, Germany, was at war with Britain and France. In 1940 we had joined Germany. And one morning, not long after that, my school friend, Dilagia, came running up to me. "Come to the corner," she urged, pulling me along with her. We swung around the corner and Dilagia stopped short, then pulled me over to the wall. "See?" she pointed.

I had never seen soldiers like these before. There were two of them standing under an elm tree studying a brochure. They wore gray-green uniforms.

"They are Germans," said Dilagia gravely.

I had heard about these soldiers from Uncle Lorenzo. He said that some years ago Il Duce had made a pact with the leader of Germany to support each other against the common enemy. The enemy, of course, was Britain and France. We were at war with them now. However, in our quiet city on the Mediterranean, it was difficult to tell that a war was on, except for the soldiers. Every time a pair would stride by, Uncle Lorenzo would shake his head, his dark blue eyes full of concern.

"That Hitler," he'd say. "I don't know about him. There are some things I don't like."

As time went on he worried more about the increasing presence of German soldiers. Papa joined him in his concern. "They tell me that they are in our other cities, too," Papa muttered.

Each passing week seemed to bring more of the gray-green uniforms. Where we had become used to seeing two in a block, we began to see four, six or more.

"We're being invaded," said Papa darkly.

They always walked in pairs. We had no real reason to be afraid of them for they were always polite, rigidly so. Even when they came into my sister Enza's grocery store, they were reserved and formal. Enza had married at sixteen and now she and her husband ran the little store. Enza told about the German soldier who came to her store. They were her best customers.

One afternoon she dropped by our house to visit. "Those Germans come in and buy the best food," she said loudly. "And what do they do with it? They ship it home to their families!"

"Maybe they come to see *you!*" laughed my brother Federico who was always one to joke. I glanced at Enza, holding back a laugh. She *was* attractive with Mama's olive skin and black eyes. Yet, even under Enza's skin I could see the blush rising. However, she chose to ignore her brother's joke. "I say," she continued, her voice rising, "if their own people don't have enough food, that they keep their men at home to raise it instead of sending them everywhere else to clutter up the streets."

Mama raised her hand. "Hush, Enza," she warned, looking anxiously over her shoulder toward the door. She always worried about the O.V.R.A. (the Fascist secret police) we heard were now everywhere. Rumors circulated about them making party opponents drink a litre of castor oil, the "Fascist baptism." Sharp concern filled her eyes. "You've got a long tongue, Enza, and it will get you into trouble," she snapped, turning back to her daughter and shaking her finger. "How many times must I tell you. . . ."

She was interrupted by Papa who hurried in the house, holding up his hand. *"Mama mia!"* he cried, "listen!" and he rushed over to the radio sitting on the windowsill and snapped it on. The announcer's voice was tense: War had been declared by Mussolini on the United States and Russia.

We stood petrified. And then we heard the words of

Mussolini himself: "This is another day of solemn decision in Italy's history and of memorable events destined to give a new course to the history of continents," he said as he explained that Italy and Germany would join Japan against the United States.

"Italians!" Mussolini called loudly over the radio, and once again I saw that bulwark of strength outlined against the afternoon sun that day we marched in the piazza. "Italians, once more arise and be worthy of this historical hour. We shall win!"

I felt so proud that I stood at attention. Then Mama called. "Rita." I turned to her. She was looking at me gravely. "Rita," she said softly, "remember that he is only a man. He is not God. And as a man. . . ."

I did not want to hear any more and turned and ran excitedly out into the street to discuss the new war with my friends.

At first the rising conflict meant little to us except more marching. It seemed there was always a parade either to see our soldiers off or to welcome visiting dignitaries. Many of these were high Nazi officials.

I'll never forget the day we paraded for Adolf Hitler. For several hours that hot afternoon we marched around and around the piazza, expecting his arrival momentarily. Finally, we were ordered to the railroad station where we assembled row upon row in parade formation. The sun set and a damp chill descended, but we continued to stand there in eager anticipation. Finally, a train wailed in the distance.

"That's it!" exclaimed the leader. As the roar of the train neared, the band struck up *Deutchland Uber Alles* and we stood at attention. We waited in breathless anticipation as the train with white flags flying thundered into the station. But it did not slacken speed!

Our band played louder as if its very volume would hold the train back. But it hurtled right through the station!

And then we saw him, standing rigidly at attention

behind the open window of the last car, his hand thrust out in the Nazi salute. Then there were only dust swirls as the German train roared on north to Rome.

But I had a brief look at the face of the man who said he would change the world. It was a cruel face, and I wondered if that was the reason why his soldiers seemed so sober. Rarely did we see them laugh as they walked down the street. Dilagia whispered that if a German soldier was responsible for an Italian girl's becoming pregnant, he would be forced to marry her by martial law. If he was married already, he would be shot.

But soon I was concerned about other matters. Federico had joined the Red Cross Ambulance Corps. And though he was fortunate to be stationed in the Naples area, we saw him very little. Many times he would be late for dinner. Even so, to Mama this was still unforgivable. But he always had a way about him. One night he rushed in twenty minutes late, washed his hands, and quickly sat down reaching for the lasagna.

"Federico!" Mama demanded.

He looked up, his hazel eyes wide with concern. "Mama, you know Luigino?"

"Yes."

"He had an accident."

"No!" gasped Mama, the milk jug poised in her hand.

"Yes," said Federico, eating quickly, "he fell under a streetcar."

"Madre mia, no!" cried Mama, clutching her heart.

Leaning over his plate, Federico added quickly: "But he got up and walked away."

"A miracle!" sighed Mama, looking up to heaven. Then the truth struck her. "You . . . !" she cried, realizing he was joking. But, of course, by this time she had forgotten her anger, and we all laughed together.

Such were dinnertimes at the Settembres. But now Federico's place at the table was often empty as he spent more and more time with the Ambulance Corps.

With his brother gone so much, Raphael—shy quiet Raphael—seemed to become more withdrawn. Like his namesake, Raphael was a wonderful artist. And now he spent his evenings working at his easel. These were quiet evenings now, I doing my homework, Raphael painting, the strains of Aïda or La Traviata drifting from Mama's phonograph. As she sat with her mending, her work-worn hands busy with yarn and her spirit lost in the music, I would think I had the most beautiful mother in the world.

And the real changes began which were to live so vividly in my mind for years to come. I first noticed the changes through Papa. Sometimes Papa would be out playing cards with his cronies. Other times he would sit under the lamp reading the newspaper, like tonight. He got up, folded the paper, and put it down. "I cannot read that news any more," he said, shaking his head. "Now they are ordering us to hate the Jews." I noticed that Papa was looking more tired, also he was getting balder. But he was still a distinguished-looking man, this Gennaro Settembre, who had traveled the world marketing his gloves. One thing about Papa, he always had time for his children. Tonight he went from Raphael to me. "Come on," he cajoled, "let's have a game of cards."

"Oh, Papa," I laughed, looking up from my homework. "You want me to get good grades, don't you? Besides," I laughed, "you know you win all the time."

It seemed like a calm, normal family scene. Yet underneath the outward calm of each of us lurked a deep fear, a sense of what was coming. Papa's comment about the news, for example. One of my friends, Carla, was Jewish. Now I was being told to hate her? Suddenly I felt I was being hemmed in. I wanted to shout out the window: "I *like* Carla! I *like* Carla!"

But in a literal sense, that would be very difficult. For now all windows had heavy blackout curtains. In school the air raid drills became more frequent. And the mounting talk of war that I heard everywhere frightened me.

One night I lay in bed not able to sleep. I remember the terrible stories about the shelling and killing related by Uncle Lorenzo from his World War I days. Mama came in to tuck me in.

"What is wrong, my *piccola bambina?*" she said.

I confessed my fears.

"Bambina," she said softly, "the lives of each of us were planned by God before we were even born. He holds our lives in His hands. But if He were to show it to you all at once, you couldn't stand it. So little by little, day by day, He gives it to us.

"But remember, *bambina,*" she added. "What is written by God cannot be erased. The good or the bad is no coincidence. Everything is for a reason.

"Che sarà, sarà," she added softly, ". . . what is to be will be." She began humming to me softly. And then she began humming louder. I wondered why. And then above her humming I heard the distant wail of sirens from the far end of the city, almost like women wailing in anguish. "Mama," I said, frightened, "you don't have to hum so I can't hear them."

Then the siren in our area started. Mama shooed me out of bed, called for Papa and Raphael, and we scurried for the cellar. As we raced through the dark kitchen, I could see through the window the skyline light up with distant flashes. Papa said they were Allied planes bombing the shipping at our port. No bombs came near us that night. However, the very next day Papa and Raphael set to work building a heavy stone and iron shelter in the cellar.

Each night the bombs marched closer to us. One morning Papa returned home from work early, his face ashen. He sat at the table over coffee a long time while Mama comforted him. When he arrived at his factory that morning, hardly one stone stood on top of another.

As the bombers roared over us more frequently, the Nazi army began to tighten its grip on the Naples populace like the closing of a vise. By the end of 1942 my school was shut down. And then one evening as we sat at supper, there was a loud knock on the door. Papa got up and opened it.

There stood a German officer.

"Gennaro Settembre?" he demanded, looking at a paper he held.

"Yes?"

"Your son, Raphael, was born in the United States."

Papa's face whitened. "But that was long ago," he said. "He has been a citizen of Italy for most of his life."

"I have orders," continued the officer, "to take your son with us as a citizen of an enemy nation."

Mama screamed and ran to Raphael, throwing her arms around him.

To Papa's protest, the officer shouted: "You are very fortunate that we are not taking your daughter, also!"

Raphael tried to soothe Mama. "It will be all right," he said. "They just want men to work in their factories." But all of us had already heard about the Nazi concentration camps.

For a long time after they left, Mama stood at the window peering through the blackout curtains. Finally, she turned and said softly: *"Che sará, sará.* One day he will come back."

I waited and waited. Each night I expected a knock on the door and to find Raphael standing there. But months went by, and he never returned.

In 1943 the bombers came over more frequently, and there was less and less of everything. Now food became rationed. But even the ration cards began to mean little. For the first time I felt hunger gnaw my insides. Mama never seemed to be hungry. What food we had she'd push at me and Papa. "You eat," she said.

Standing in line for bread was an ordeal. Sometimes it would be three or four hours while we fidgeted and waited. At first we complained. But that did no good. So we just waited silently. The worst was when you could smell the fragrance of fresh bread coming from the front of the line. It would drive me crazy. And then, so often, I would reach the front of the line to be told, "All out." Crying and complaining touched no one. All we could do was to find another line, hoping there would be some left.

How was I to know that the little baby, Anna Marie, who was born to my sister, Enza, was to play such a role in circumstances that shaped my attitudes? It was really because of the baby that we spent that fateful night in Bagnoli. Enza's husband was in the army, and she and the baby, Anna Marie, now seven months old, moved to Bagnoli, a small seaside town outside of Naples. Alone with the baby, Enza begged Mama and me to visit. We very much wanted to see them so we traveled there. We flipped a coin to see who would get to stay with Enza, for her house was very small. I won. Which is how it happened that I was with Enza, one night, and Mama was in a nearby hotel.

Early in the morning I was awakened by the sound of distant planes and the thud of bombs. They came closer. I sat up in bed. Enza awoke and ran for her baby, climbing back into bed holding her. Now the bombs were striking close, as the house shuddered and pieces of plaster fell onto the bed. Enza held her baby and I kneeled at the bedside praying, a blanket over us all to help protect us against the plaster. Now the floor heaved beneath us like the deck of a pitching ship. Once, during a lull, I lifted the blanket and peeked. Through the window I could see bright flares floating down from the sky. The whole village seemed to be in flames. And then a horrifying sound made us lock ourselves into each other's arms. A screeching howl I had never heard before, louder and louder, followed by a tremendous thud outside that rocked the house.

"Let's get out of here," I yelled, scrambling for the door. As I opened it, I shrieked in terror. In the light of the burning town, a tremendous gray form loomed at the door step. It was a giant unexploded bomb. Even with its head buried deep in the earth, its fins towered over me. I shrank back in terror and slammed the door. We climbed through a broken window, and with Enza holding her baby and both of us crying, we picked our way through debris-filled streets to the hotel where Mama was.

In the early red firelight, shadowy figures whimpered as they searched among the ruins. We rounded a corner and stopped still, our hands to our mouths. There was nothing left of the hotel!

Mama must be under that rubble! We climbed to the top of the smoking ruins, and started pulling at the stones. And then we heard a familiar voice shouting behind us. We turned. It was Mama!

She explained between taking heavy breaths: "During the night . . . something . . . told me to leave the hotel . . . I gathered my clothes . . . went out . . . stayed in a little room in a house down the street.

"I'm sure . . ." she gasped, "it was God speaking to me."

Something happened to me that morning. Always in the past I had paid little attention to Mama's talk of God and religion. But this was something different. Mama *believed* so completely that God protected her, that He apparently actually had!

That day we tried to leave Bagnoli. We huddled at the side of the dusty road trying to get a ride on one of the trucks that groaned toward Naples with the wounded. As we peered down the road, Mama stiffened, clutched my arm and pointed to two weary figures trudging toward us. It was Papa and Federico

wearing his Red Cross uniform. In Naples they had
heard that Bagnoli had been destroyed. Federico wasn't
able to get an ambulance. But by begging rides and
walking, he and poor little Papa fought their way many
miles to us. It was a joyful reunion.

"The good Lord has spared us," said Mama gratefully. "After tonight I shall never be afraid, even during
the bombing. He is *always* with us." *Well,* I said to
myself, *maybe He is at that!*

From then on, it was only His Spirit that day who
sustained us. Naples was completely pockmarked with
bomb craters. We had to pick our way down the street
to avoid falling into the gaping holes in which broken
pipes dripped and steamed.

All of Naples' utilities were destroyed and no longer
would water come out of our faucets. There was only
one way to get it. Crawl down into a bomb crater, and
collect it in a bucket from one of the dripping pipes.

I'll never forget the first night I had to do this. Both
Enza and little Anna Marie were sick, and since that
night Papa and Federico were away, it was up to me
to get the water.

"Leave the door open, Mama," I called fearfully
over my shoulder as I stepped out into the dark, de-
serted street.

"Honey, we can't," said Mama, "the blackout, remember?"

I walked across the mist-slickened cobblestones, my
heart pounding. Somewhere in the blackness before me
yawned the crater. Even from where I stood, terrified,
I could hear the scuffling. I knew what it was—giant
rats that roamed these craters searching for water. Some
people said if they were cornered they would leap for
your throat.

I inched forward, and finally came to the bomb
crater. I put the water pail down, not able to bring
myself to climb down into that terrifying pit which

yawned before me, illuminated only by starlight. Far down in it I could hear the water dripping from the broken pipe. I looked up to the stars. And then I remembered Mama, and the way she said God was always with us.

Picking up the bucket, I edged down into the pit, dislodging chunks of rubble which clattered down, splashing in the puddles below. I made my way to the pipe and hung the bucket over its lip. As I waited for the pail to fill, I could feel small malevolent eyes on me. But I was able to stand there until the pail was brimfull, for I kept looking up to the stars, *His* stars.

Back at our house we had to boil the water for now the horrible disease of typhoid fever stalked Naples. Even so, a few days later Anna Marie became sick. She cried and cried, then became strangely silent, her little eyes staring at the ceiling. One morning I was awakened by screaming and moaning. Mama came into my room, her eyes dark with grief. "Little Anna Marie has gone to heaven," she said.

The pain of our grief was intensified as the fever then struck Mama, Papa, Enza, and me. Our house was quarantined. Federico had the illness when he was a child, and perhaps this saved him, for fortunately he was able to care for us. From time to time, Mama would tell us, "Let us sing." And we'd sing together in feeble, cracking voices. "Singing is good for the soul," she would say determinedly.

"But Mama," I complained between parched lips. "How can you want to sing at a time like this?"

"Rita, as long as we're alive, we have hope. Come . . ." and we'd sing, even old popular songs like *"L'una Furtiva Lacrima"* ("A Furtive Tear").

Finally, the disease with its aches, nosebleeds, and rash left our house. But it only set the stage for a new horror.

We did not get much news of the war, only that there was terrible fighting everywhere. And then in July 1943, rumors flew that the Allies had landed forces in Sicily.

Meanwhile, the Allied bombers had started dropping new kinds of missiles—paper leaflets. Uncle Lorenzo brought one over to Papa. It spoke to the Italians, saying, ". . . the time has come for you to decide whether Italians shall die for Mussolini and Hitler, or live for Italy and civilization."

Uncle Lorenzo said quietly, almost to himself. "I hear rumors of rebellion among high government leaders." He said it almost in a tone of hope. The corruption which had been buried so long in the Fascist regime was now bubbling to the surface. Everyone knew that Mussolini, a married man, was living with his mistress, Clara Petacci. And it was now apparent that there were no laws for him to obey—moral or otherwise—his only criterion seeming to be that the end justifies the means.

"And we allowed it all to happen," said Uncle Lorenzo, sadly shaking his head. "We allowed it to happen."

In July Sicily fell to the Allies. And now I heard something on the street I could hardly believe. I rushed home. "Mama! Papa!" I called, "did you hear? They say that King Victor Emmanuel has had Mussolini arrested by the carabinieri!" The carabinieri police had always been loyal to the king.

They had been listening to the radio, and Papa looked up and nodded. "Yes, thank God," he said. "And now we have a new premier, Senor Badoglio." He sighed. "Maybe he can save what's left of Italy."

Then more news! On September 3, 1943, our country surrendered to the Allies. The feeling on the streets was one of intense relief, even though Mussolini had escaped and was running his own puppet government up north.

But as the Allies landed at Salerno on the coast just below us, the Nazis fell back, entrenching themselves in Naples. All day and all night we could hear the endless roaring as truck after truck came into the city loaded with tired, nervous troops.

And now the Nazis turned on us. First, they rounded up the Jews and sent them away to concentration camps. We had never really paid attention to the anti-Semitic role we were supposed to play. But now, Naples had become a giant prison. And soon we realized that our guards had gone mad. Perhaps the madness stemmed from fear-filled soldiers who knew their Allied pursuers were approaching from Salerno. But all civilization was suspended.

The Nazis took over the courts, and the judges sat with guns at their backs. Federico came home one night in tears. He told how one man was arguing with a guard about something, and evidently pushed his case too far. There was a quick explosion of a rifle and the argument was settled.

Through underground channels we heard Premier Badoglio's order: "Fight the Germans in every way, everywhere, and all the time."

And now Naples began to fight back. Strange men slipped into our house at night carrying guns. They were partisans, fighting Germans. But the price was dear.

One night a German soldier was shot in the street. The next day the Nazis rounded up fifty Neopolitan men, carried them outside the city in trucks, and shot them all. This happened again and again.

In October, Italy declared war on Germany and Japan. That very day the Nazis swooped through the streets, rounding up all the men and boys they could find, packed them into freight cars, and sent them to Germany. They left from the very same depot where we had stood just a few years ago with our band, to honor the Nazi leader.

What happened then has gone down in history as The Last Four Days of Naples. With the Allied army only a few miles down the coast, the Nazis prepared to leave. But before doing so, they determined to destroy everything possible. The harbor was demolished, entire city blocks were dynamited, libraries burned. It seemed as if the very winds of hell blew down the streets, damaging even our glorious cathedral dedicated to Saint Januarius, patron of Naples.

We Settembres huddled in our home as explosions rocked the neighborhood hour after hour. A curfew was set and all were forbidden to enter the streets. A Nazi tank squatted at virtually every street corner. Anything seen moving during curfew hours was cut down by machine-gun bullets.

Not everyone understood the curfew hours. One morning, as an early mist curled up from the paving stones, we heard someone leave the house next door. Mama looked at me in consternation; it was still curfew time. She pulled back the window curtain and gasped: "It is Geraldo!" He was a fifteen-year-old boy who lived next door. Suddenly we heard a burst of machine-gun fire, then an anguished wail as Geraldo's mother flew into the street. None of us could stand it and despite the danger, opened our door and followed her. She was leaning over Geraldo's crumpled body, sobbing, her skirts soaked with his blood. Papa, Federico and two other men lifted the slight body up and carried it to his house.

Now we Neapolitans began starving in our homes. Our food dwindled, until one morning Mama held up a little sack of small potatoes. "This is all we have left," she said. We waited until noon that day to eat. We all sat down at the table. She took out two potatoes, sliced each in half, giving a half to Papa, Enza, Federico, and myself. Slowly I chewed it, savoring each morsel. I was almost done with mine when I looked at Mama. She was sitting with her head bowed, quietly giving thanks. Then it struck me. Mama had not taken *any* potato! Here we had all reached for ours, and were greedily eating, forgetting even to thank our Lord who had provided it.

I told Papa and the others. That evening when we ate our second half, we made sure Mama got a whole one. Then we all bowed our heads and thanked Him for His providence.

Not all of the Neapolitans fared as well. During non-curfew time, I slipped out to visit my friend Maria who had been sick. I brought a potato with me with Mama's blessing. When I reached Maria's house, her mother met me at the door crying and shaking her head. I looked past her and saw on Maria's bed a form covered with a sheet. Malnutrition makes tuberculosis work very fast.

Meanwhile, men and boys continued slipping out into the streets to fight back. Sometimes they caught soldiers alone in the dark, other times they were reduced to throwing rocks at tanks. These fighters included the *Scugnizzi,* the nickname given to the little homeless boys who lived by their wits, begging, shoe-shining. One night they formed a band and broke into a city police station. Armed with police rifles and pistols, they openly faced the tanks and machine gunners. Many of their souls were in heaven long before their little bodies were carried off of the blood-stained streets.

The fifth morning we awoke to a strange presence outside. For a moment we could not understand what it was. Then we realized. It was silence. There was no sound at all. The Nazis had left on their flight north.

We crept out into the streets to find desolation. Buildings were still crumbling and bloated, stinking bodies lay everywhere. We came across the body of one little Scugnizzi face down against a building, his short pants stained with blood. Mama and I prayed for Jesus to take his soul into heaven.

Through it all a new kind of love grew between us —a love far more important than food. All of us found

ourselves close to God. We knew He was feeding us
with something far different from the bread we had
once thought was most important.

For a few brief days we lived in that strange inter-
lude that exists between the time of a departing army
and the arrival of a new force. It was a time of looting,
of rampaging criminals the Nazis had vengefully let
loose.

"This is what happens when we let a godless man
take over," said Mama.

"Yes," agreed Papa, "and I hear rumors that up in
Verona Mussolini had many members of his own
Grand Council including his own son-in-law, exe-
cuted."

"Well," added Mama, looking out the window, "we
are all reaping the harvest of such ones. They are not
ruled by God." I remember saying to myself that as
long as I lived I would help support men who believed
in God.

I had become sick again with a relapse of the fever.
While lying in bed, I heard the grinding noise of large
trucks and loud cheering in the streets. Mama looked
out the window. "They are the Americans!" she cried
excitely and ran out to wave. She came back laughing, carrying a large loaf of bread. "A truck full of
soldiers were passing out bread to everyone," she cried,
tears of joy streaming down her face.

Turbulent times followed, times of hunger and the
ever-present fear that Nazi bombers would now attack
us to take vengeance. But under the Allied Army of
Occupation, we had hoped that the war would soon
end, and we could begin living again.

The war did finally end throughout Europe in early
1945 with the collapse of Germany. But something far
more significant collapsed for me at about the same
time.

Through underground channels we had kept track
of Mussolini after he was deposed. We learned of his

puppet Fascist government up north. And then we heard he had again become a prisoner.

One morning while walking through the piazza, I noticed crowds of people gathered around the news stands. "What is all the excitement about?" I asked a friend who I happened to meet. Her eyes widened. "Haven't you heard?" she cried, "He is dead."

"Who is dead?"

"Mussolini. He and his mistress were trying to escape to Switzerland and the partisans caught them near Como. They shot both of them."

I rushed to the newsstand, then wished that I hadn't. There, taking over the front page of the paper, was a grotesque photograph of the bodies of Mussolini and Clara Petacci hanging in a piazza in Milan. I pushed my fists into my eyes trying to blot out the terrible picture. And then other pictures came before me, of a proud man proclaiming an eternal regime, of a proud man looking down from my schoolroom wall over the words: MUSSOLINI IS ALWAYS RIGHT. The mixture of pictures swam together as Mama's and Papa's words echoed within me: "Remember, Rita, he is a man, not God." And, "A people gets what it allows."

Yes, a people gets what it allows. Mussolini had promised us much. But in blindly following him we had not looked to see whom *he* had followed. No one but himself. One by one our personal freedoms were taken away until—too late—we found ourselves locked in with a system not based on the truth and light of God, but on the dark and pragmatic standards of the prince of the earth.

It was a truth I would never forget.

Now the war's thundering echoes faded as people tried to pick up their lives where they had been so many years ago. Papa found some of his old employees, obtained the use of another building, and began making gloves again. As months went by, Italian soldiers plus men who had been taken prisoner by the Nazis began to drift back. Each time Papa saw one he would question him about Raphael. But all would shake their heads. By now we thought he was dead—except Mama. Even though it had been over three years since he was taken away, she would smile and say, *"Che sará, sará."*

But each evening, Papa would settle himself at the table and sigh, "Well, I met another soldier today. He had no idea what happened to Raphael."

But one night, I looked up to see Papa peeking into the door with a strange expression on his face. Then he came in, walked up to Mama, and kissed her saying, "Assunta, I have a surprise for you."

She turned and looked at him, her eyes steady, hands clasped before her, "Raphael is back," she said quietly.

Poor Papa. He so much had wanted to surprise her. For a moment his face fell, then he rushed to the door calling, "Raphael, come in! Come in!"

We all gasped in shock. Was this thin, bearded scarecrow with hollow eyes and ragged clothes our Raphael? But as soon as he kissed us, we knew. There was the same laugh, the same light in his eyes.

Papa told us how as he was walking home that evening he saw a man obviously returning from prison camp. "He had such a long beard and was covered with dust," laughed Papa. "I asked him what camp he had come from. When he told me, I said, 'But I have a son there. Raphael Settembre. Perhaps you have heard of him.' The bearded one began to cry. 'Papa,' he said, 'it's me, Raphael!' " They both had changed so much neither recognized the other.

Again we laughed and all tried to hug him at once.

Mama cooked a celebration dinner, but it was hardly touched as we listened to Raphael tell how he had escaped from the German concentration camp with the help of partisans, and then crossed the border into Italy.

He then looked at Mama, love shining in his eyes, and said, "I could always feel your prayers, Mama."

Raphael had come home none too soon. Within three months, Papa was dead from a heart attack. For weeks I mourned and stayed inside our house. Enza and her husband had set up housekeeping elsewhere, the boys were out working. Mama felt it was too lonely for me to stay inside, and urged me to go out and see my friends. By now, many of my girl friends were dating soldiers. Finally, I began accompanying them to the American servicemen's club. After a few visits I began to enjoy it. It was fun. Music, laughing, I even learned to do the funny American jitterbug.

And then one night I found myself dancing with the tallest man I had ever seen. He was six feet, four inches, and as we moved across the floor to the strains of "Everywhere I Look I See Your Face," I thought he was the most wonderful man I had ever met.

His name was Leverett Warren. He had dark hair, quiet hazel eyes, and he was a staff sergeant in charge of the servicemen's club. Each time I returned, I looked forward to talking with him. His Italian, though limited, was enough for us, especially since he really didn't talk that much. He did tell me about the place where he was from. Boston. "You know," he said, "where Paul Revere lived?" I didn't know what he was talking about. He was a very quiet man. After a few weeks he asked me for a date, and soon we were going to the beach regularly to swim.

One night he held me close and whispered in English, "Rita, I love you."

On our next date I presented him with a dozen eggs. He looked at them incredulously. "Why?" he asked in Italian.

"Isn't that what you wanted?" I inquired. And then, he laughed and laughed as he realized what had happened. The Italian word for eggs is *uove* and in the Neapolitan dialect it is pronounced *luv*.

We went steady for six months, and then Leverett proposed marriage. Our priest married us on July 28, 1946. Since Leverett was Protestant, we could not get married in our church. But the priest agreed to perform the ceremony in our home. Mama had Raphael build an altar in the house and he decorated it beautifully. "At least my daughter will be married before an altar," she said.

All the family was there, except, of course, for poor Papa. Uncle Lorenzo took Papa's place and gave me away. Before the ceremony as we waited in the bedroom, he took my hand and gave me his blessing. "Remember, my little Rita, when I used to sing you to sleep at night?"

"Yes, Uncle Lorenzo," I replied, "and I will always remember *'Su per monti noi marceremo,'* the Alpinists' song."

"Never forget, my little one," he said gently, as he pressed a check into my hand as a wedding present, "what I have told you. It is better to live one day as a lion than a hundred days as a sheep." Inside I smiled. Uncle Lorenzo was quoting one of the favorite sayings of the old regime. But still, it was good advice I felt.

After the ceremony, Leverett and I honeymooned on the Isle of Capri where in a little boat we slipped into the grotto. Inside it was another world, silent and mysterious. The water glowed with an ethereal blue-green illumination. I dipped my hand into it and then shook off diamondlike droplets. I leaned back on Leverett and felt as if I was in heaven. Once I had placed all my security in a national leader. But now in the arms of my husband I felt real security. I would never have to worry again.

And again, I would be shown how wrong I was.

3.

In a New Land

Christmas 1946. A gray drizzle slicked the streets of Florence where Leverett and I now lived. He had been transferred here shortly after our wedding. He had twenty-four hours' leave for the holiday, and Mama and Federico had traveled up from Naples to spend it with us. It was the saddest Christmas of my life. Leverett had received orders to return to the United States. We would leave Italy for America the day after tomorrow.

How can I forget the sorrow in Mama's eyes as we parted that next day? "I'll never see you again, my little daughter," she said softly as I clung to her.

"Oh, Mama, don't say that," I cried, drawing back and trying to laugh. I looked at her as she stood at the end of the hallway in which we were saying good-bye. She was still in mourning for Papa. But even in black, with the way her hair was pushed back and the bit of lace around her neck, she was beautiful.

"Oh, Mama," I sighed, "I wish I were an artist. I'd paint you right now." I stood looking at her a long time, etching her face into my memory.

"You'll be coming to America to see us soon," I said, fighting the cold feeling inside me that Mama's statement about not seeing me again was prophetic.

"Take care of *piccola bambina,*" she whispered. I was pregnant.

"Mama, when he is born you shall come to see him,"

I tried to laugh bravely. Inside I cried. Brother Federico held me tight. "Good-bye, *piccola sorella,* my little
sister," he choked, wiping his eyes. Then he smiled.
"Say, I will call you sometime over the telephone, and
sing a song for you."

I stood at the window of our apartment, watching
Mama and Federico get into the taxi that would take
them to the railroad station. Federico got Mama settled,
waved up at me, and the cab disappeared into the gray
mist. To keep busy, I spent the next several hours pack-
ing the new suitcases my husband had purchased for
me at the Post Exchange.

Two days later, Leverett and I were aboard the big
army transport ship as it slowly moved out of the
harbor. Dozens of war brides lined the rail; we were
all crying as we watched the mountains of Italy fade
into the horizon. None of us really knew what kind of
a country we were headed for. And I'm sure that most
of us felt that we would never see our parents, brothers,
and sisters again.

Leverett wasn't feeling well, and I stood at the rail
alone. As the ocean mist mingled with the tears streaming down my face, I ached for the comforting embrace
of my husband. Then I felt a hand tentatively touch my
shoulder. I looked up; it was a corporal and his wife
who had been standing at the rail next to me. Both
looked at me with compassion, and they drew me over
to them. It was good to feel a comforting arm while
we watched the hills of homeland disappear into the
mist.

For the full thirteen days of the crossing I had little
time to think of my homeland. They were thirteen days
of horror as the ship pitched and rolled in an endless
Atlantic winter storm. I became so ill that the doctor
was afraid I would lose my baby. As I lay on the bunk,
my face pressed into the cold metal wall of the cabin,
I put my life and my baby's life into God's hands.

Finally, I heard people talking about seeing land and
Leverett helped me to the deck. The United States did

not at all look like what I had expected. I had looked forward to seeing giant skyscrapers and a towering Statue of Liberty. But all I could see were tiny boxlike houses on a low shoreline. Leverett explained that this was Long Island, and that our ship would be docking in Brooklyn.

I gazed on the gray shoreline wondering what lay ahead. I felt I had left the war, hunger, and persecution far behind. But I had no idea of the harrowing experiences that were in store for me, a series of experiences which in my helplessness would teach me the real meaning of complete dependence on God.

We had planned to go directly to Leverett's home in Boston, where his parents were expecting us. However, all of us had to go first through processing and medical examinations before being cleared.

I was concerned about the baby after that terrible voyage. But, as it turned out, Leverett was the one we had to worry about. Back in Italy, he had a serious case of scarlet fever. Whether or not this was responsible, we never knew, but the physical examination indicated that something was wrong with Leverett's heart.

He sat down next to me and squeezed my shoulder after telling me, for I had broken down and cried. "It's only a little murmur," he said, gently. "But they have ordered me to go to Walter Reed Hospital in Washington, D.C."

"I'll go with you," I blurted. I had a horror of being alone in this strange country.

"No, Honey," he said. "You can't do that. I don't know how long they'll keep me there, maybe weeks or even a month or two. You'd be all alone.

"Look," he continued, "it will be better for you and the baby to go right up to Mom and Dad in Boston. They'll take care of you."

I said nothing; a lump was growing in my throat.

"The Red Cross lady said that they would see that you get on the right train for Boston," he added.

A few hours later, my heart breaking, I kissed him

goodbye. As usual, Leverett had to lean down to me, and I had to step on my tiptoes to reach him. I waved feebly as I watched him disappear through the door.

A kindly Red Cross lady, who looked like Aunt Maria and spoke Italian, took me to a dormitory where I would spend the night. "We'll take you to the station tomorrow, dear," she said, "and put you on the right train. We have called your mother-in-law, and she will be waiting at the station."

"But how will I know when the train gets to Boston?"

"Don't worry; the conductor will tell you. Besides," she laughed, "it's not easy to miss. The trip ends at Boston; the train doesn't go any farther."

She wished me good-night and I fell on my cot sobbing. Here I had been in America only one day and my husband was gone.

The next morning the Red Cross lady drove me into the city to the railroad station. And I saw that the buildings in New York *did* reach the sky. But I didn't see much else. There was so much noise, too many flashing lights, crowds of people rushing by. Soon the Red Cross lady was saying good-bye. "Remember," she said as she settled me into my seat on the coach, "your mother-in-law will be waiting for you when you get into Boston." Then she left and I was sitting on the train looking at the ticket she had given me. I could spell out the word: B-O-S-T-O-N. Carefully, I said it over and over again. Other than a few words Leverett had taught me, I could speak no English.

What kind of city was Boston? I had a strange feeling that in some way my destiny was to be linked with it. Leverett said that Boston was where the American Revolution had started. I looked forward to seeing it. I remembered from history a little something of how the American people fought for independence, and then developed a system of rules by which to govern themselves, based on something called a *Constitution*. I was not too clear about it, because they began to teach history a little differently in our school after Il Duce came to power. But whatever had happened in this city back then sounded good to me because, after the past years, I had come to know too well what could happen when power was concentrated in the hands of a few people.

I opened my purse to make sure I had the little photograph of my mother-in-law that Leverett had given me.

The train sped through the city, villages, and countryside and then along the ocean. I looked past the wintry beaches out into the gray Atlantic, and took comfort in knowing that far on the other side of the ocean was a little house on a cobblestone street in which Mama was probably sitting even now, praying for me and the life I was starting in this new land.

Each station we stopped at I would ask the conductor, "Boston?" He would shake his head and say something I could not understand.

Finally, after several hours the train seemed to be entering a big city and traveling slower. Large buildings and walls now crowded the track. Then the train slowed to a stop at a station. A lot of people got off. I started getting nervous, and turned to a man reading a newspaper who sat across the aisle from me.

"Boston?" I asked, touching his shoulder. He looked up from his paper and nodded. Quickly, I gathered my two suitcases and got off the train.

There were a few people waiting on the platform but none of them looked like Leverett's mother. The train was gone, and most of the people were gone. I set my suitcases down and stood there, feeling very alone. A light snow began to fall and I shivered. Naples was never like this.

Perhaps his mother was late? I sat down on my suitcases and waited. A half-hour went by and still no one came. I hugged myself trying to keep warm. Finally, I could stand it no longer. I picked up my suitcases and

walked up to the street. A taxi was sitting there. I remembered that Leverett had said his parents lived in a
neighborhood called Parker Hill.

I walked over to the cab. "Hello," I said in Italian,
"can you take me to Parker Hill?"

He looked at me in puzzlement, then held his hands
out, palms up, indicating that he couldn't understand me.

Suddenly, I felt so alone. My husband was in a
hospital far off somewhere in this vast land. And I was
lost in a strange city where no one could speak Italian.
I wanted to cry. I turned to pick up my suitcases, and
walk back to the station when the driver called something. I turned back to him and he was pointing to my
suitcases. I saw what he meant: the luggage tag on
which Leverett had written his home address. I picked
up the suitcase and showed the driver the tag. He
nodded, and opened the door for me to get in. We drove
through streets now filling with snow. I became frightened as the cab slid and swerved. Finally we stopped
and the driver pointed to a tall two-story building. He
helped me out of the cab, and carried my suitcases up
the snowy steps. I smiled: *"Grazie,"* and asked
"Quanto costa?"

He said something I couldn't understand. I smiled
again, shaking my head, *"Non capisco."*

He held up two fingers. Ah. I looked in my purse
at the American money Leverett had given me. Would
I ever figure out this strange-looking paper? It was all
the same size, and each looked the same, unlike Italian
money which came in different sizes and colors. Finally, I found two papers that had the number *one* in
the corners, and handed them to the driver. He smiled,
tipped his hat, and left.

Well, I thought, feeling a little surge of confidence, I
had handled *that* all right. I turned to the door. There
was the name *Warren* above one of the two bells. I

pressed the button. No one answered. I pressed it again. Now the snow was falling harder; it was getting into my eyes and hair. Still no one answered. Then I heard footsteps behind the other door and it opened. A pretty young woman said something in English and smiled. All I could understand was "Mrs. Warren?" I nodded. She picked up my bags, and ushered me upstairs to her apartment, motioned for me to take off my coat, and held out a chair. I was grateful to sit down. Then she pointed downstairs and said, "Leverett's mother." I smiled and nodded. She pointed to the clock, indicating I should wait, and offered me coffee.

In about an hour her doorbell rang. My hostess went downstairs and I could hear excited talk. Someone called me, and I walked downstairs, and there stood a tall gray-haired woman, who smiled and held out her hand. It was Leverett's mother.

Later, I learned that I had got off the train at Back Bay Station which is several miles before the end of the line at the big terminal called South Station. Mrs. Warren had been waiting for me all that time at South Station.

For three months I stayed with Leverett's mother and stepfather. His mother was quiet and reserved, while his stepfather was jolly and outgoing.

The first Sunday I was there, Mother Warren took me to the Catholic church in the neighborhood. I wondered how she happened to be Catholic when her son wasn't. I was glad she was a believer. She was also a very practical person. From the first day she began teaching me English. As we did the dishes, she would hand me a piece of dishware to dry, saying, "Cup," over and over. Everything I touched she would give the English word: *potato, glass, water*. And then one day when the weather was becoming warmer, she took me to the window and pointed at a bird I had never seen before. "R o b i n," she said.

Within a few weeks I was able to speak some English. One of my first questions was how come Leverett was Protestant.

"Oh," she said, looking a bit embarrassed, "so am I." And then I discovered that she had taken me to the Catholic church realizing that I would be more at home there. Up until then, I had always considered Mrs. Warren to be a bit formidable, she was often so stern and quiet. But now I learned that crusty exteriors hide a compassionate nature.

In the meantime, letters came from Leverett at Walter Reed Hospital. Since his condition involved his heart the doctor wanted to keep him under observation a while longer.

As the weather continued to warm, I would sit on the Warren's porch, wearing a heavy sweater, as it was still sharp outside. I enjoyed watching the neighborhood children play games on the sidewalk and noticed all of them seemed to have bicycles. Across the tree-lined street was the New England Baptist Hospital. I was impressed by the many fine-looking automobiles that pulled up to the entrance and wondered if the people that got out of them were government bigwigs. In Italy the only people who traveled in large cars were high officials.

"No, Rita," explained Mrs. Warren. "In this country many people own cars like that."

I looked at the cars, and the children with all their expensive toys, and thought how often in Italy we used to laugh about the people who went to America because they heard the streets were full of money. We knew that wasn't true. But I had to admit that everyone here seemed to have a lot more to show for their labors.

Later in the spring two wonderful things happened. Leverett was discharged from the hospital and came home. And our son Robert was born. A Caesarean birth.

Now we *had* to find an apartment. We applied to a nearby housing project, but the man in charge just shook his head. I sat on the porch wondering what to do and the words of my mother came to me, "Rita, when you need something important, see the top man." It was advice I was to put to good use in the coming years again and again.

I asked my father-in-law who our "top man" was. "We have a very good Senator, Chester Dolan," he said. I went to Mr. Dolan's office. I tried and tried to explain my problem, but my English was so poor I almost gave up. Then Senator Dolan came to my rescue. He had served in Naples with the U.S. Army Air Corps in World War II and he could speak some Italian. He was delighted to talk with someone from Naples. Through his help, Leverett and I were able to move into an apartment project in East Boston.

It was in these years that I got my second papers, and became a full-fledged American citizen. I'll never forget that day when I stood before a judge in the courtroom and with my right hand raised, solemnly swore to support the Constitution of the United States of America. I had no idea then how deeply I would get involved in this pledge!

Leverett started working as a garage mechanic, earning forty dollars per week. And each week I was able to send a little money to Mama in Naples. A year went by and we celebrated Bobby's first birthday. But instead of the year bringing Leverett and me closer, we seemed to drift apart. At night I would lie awake in bed and worry. Was I not the same girl he thought he was marrying in Italy? But then, I thought, his mother seemed to have this same coolness of nature. Perhaps it was the "Boston reserve" I kept hearing about. On the other hand, I was still such a child. Would I ever grow up and become a real American wife? I wondered.

In 1948 my brother Raphael, who we all thought had been lost in the war, came to the United States for a visit. He stayed with us for a few weeks. Raphael and I had great fun talking over old times, and I particularly enjoyed hearing how well Mama seemed to be doing. She had her house redecorated, and now had an electric phonograph. Finally, when it came time for him to return to Italy, Raphael smiled. "You know, Rita, I like it here. I may be back some day." And then he added quietly, "But there is one thing I don't understand. I don't see you and Leverett going to church. What is wrong?"

I changed the subject. But it was true. All this time Leverett and I never went to church. Oh, once in a while I would slip into the local Catholic church. But church, as a rule, never seemed to have a place in our family's routine.

Not until I was two months pregnant with my second child did I realize how far I had drifted away from the Lord. One night I awakened with severe pains in my back and side and was rushed to the hospital. It was diagnosed as a kidney infection. Because of the infection and the extensive medication given to me for it, the doctor felt certain that I would lose the baby.

"I wouldn't worry too much about losing it, Mrs. Warren," he said gently. "After all, you are only two months pregnant. Moreover, I would be concerned about the fetus; the medicine may have affected it adversely."

But I desperately wanted to keep this child.

"All right," said the doctor. He recommended that I stay in bed for several days, moving as little as possible, until the danger of losing it passed. I did just that, and for the first time in months I began to pray again. "Please, God, save my baby."

Seven months later my second baby was born, again by Caesarean. After I left the delivery room and was back in my bed, I called for my baby. The nurses were strangely silent. Finally, my doctor came in and sat down at the side of my bed. "You have a daughter," he said, "and she is beautiful. However," and he lowered his voice and took my hand, "she is very small, only five pounds, and we are going to keep her in an incubator for a while. She seems to have trouble breathing."

My hand flew to my mouth and I sat up. "I want to see her right away," I pleaded. Leverett arrived. He helped the nurse get me into a wheel chair. The doctor came with us. "I must prepare you beforehand for something else," he said. I was filled with fear. Leverett took my hand. "Your baby has deformed hands and feet," the doctor said gently. "But please do not feel too badly about it," he quickly added as I stared at him in disbelief. "This is something a good plastic surgeon can easily fix later." Then he opened the door and we went into the room where the baby lay. She looked so pitiful in the glass incubator. I wanted to take her and hold her and not let her go. Leverett and I named her Anita.

Then, a few days later, I got the full report they had been afraid to give me earlier. The doctors had little hope that Anita would live.

"There are so many internal maladjustments," my doctor said. "Please, Mrs. Warren, don't feel badly if she doesn't make it." He took my hand, and added, "Believe me, it might be better for everyone."

I couldn't accept that. I couldn't let it happen. I prayed for Anita daily. The tiny baby surprised the doctors as she continued to hang on to life. Finally, in a few weeks, they had to admit that she might live after all. Leverett and I took her home, and I couldn't be prouder of any child. Leverett's mother and stepfather were especially pleased to have a granddaughter.

But this was only the beginning of a series of crises. When Anita was three months old, she was stricken with influenza. Her temperature soared to 105 degrees. I called our priest to have her blessed, and then Leverett and I stood over her crib watching her tiny form as she gasped for air. I prayed as I never had before. "Jesus, dear Jesus," I pleaded. "I'll go back to church every Sunday. I'll turn myself over to You. But please, help this little one of Yours to live."

The doctor came, poked around, shook his head, used a lot of big words, and left. I stayed at Anita's side, finally falling asleep over the crib. The next morning I awakened with a start. With a thumping heart, I raised myself and looked down at the baby. Her tiny hazel eyes were wide open. Hesitantly, I touched her little forehead. It was cool. She seemed to smile at my touch. I broke into tears thanking Jesus for what He had done. Excitedly, I called the doctor. He came over in his car, examined her, then turned to me. He was pleased. "Rita, I couldn't tell you last night," he said, "but I really thought your child would die. She's a mighty lucky little girl."

"Lucky?" I said. "I prayed to our Lord Jesus."

He slowly shook his head, his eyes on Anita. "Rita, I'm a Jew. But I must say that whoever you prayed to has certainly helped. It was a miracle."

One thing became apparent. Anita was to bring me much closer to God. How I was to need that closeness, not only for Anita but for the other children I was to strive for in the years ahead! At six months I noticed that Anita couldn't do many of the things my son Bobby did at that age. She couldn't focus her eyes, and seldom smiled directly at me. Even when she was a year old, she didn't stand. At two years the doctor put her through a series of tests to find out what was wrong. The day came when he called Leverett and me into his office. "Mr. and Mrs. Warren," he said gravely, "it's difficult for me to tell you this, but your Anita is mentally retarded." Then he read a long list of the other things that were wrong with our baby. Congenital abnormalities affected almost every part of her body.

In August 1952, Anita had plastic surgery on her deformed feet. Finally, she was able to walk. Whenever he could, little Bobby would try to help her, but she stumbled easily. In one bad fall she seriously injured her face, which meant still another operation; this time it was plastic surgery on her nose.

She could still say only one word: *Mama*. All of us —Leverett, his parents, and I—would talk to her constantly, but she would never try to answer. At the age of five, Anita was not yet toilet-trained. Our pediatrician tried to encourage us, explaining that it would take a long time before we'd see any noticeable changes in her.

In 1956, at the age of six, Anita was given psychological tests. She scored a Stanford-Binet mental age of two years and seven months, giving her an IQ rating of 41. The doctor, after reading me the report, sat silent for a moment, turning a pencil over and over in his hand. "Mrs. Warren," he finally said, "if you wish, Anita is eligible for immediate admission to a state institution. It might be better for her and . . . ."

I leaned forward in my chair. "No, Doctor," I exclaimed. "I could never do that. I love her and she needs me."

"Well," he continued, "you must think of the rest of your family." I was thinking of them. I was remembering a recent afternoon when I was out hanging clothes and overheard a conversation take place on the sidewalk. Bobby had taken Anita out to play. A new child in the neighborhood came over and as Anita awkwardly pushed a tricycle, the new child began to laugh and point at "that dumb kid."

My heart caught and I froze, my hand holding a clothespin. Anger surged through me, and I grasped the clothesline tightly to keep from rushing out to the defense of my child.

But I didn't need to. Bobby turned to the new child and with his little voice full of concern, said, "Don't make fun of Anita. It's not her fault. She's just different from us, that's all." He walked over to her and put his arm around her: "I love her, Mama loves her, and God loves her."

I stood with my hand on the clothesline, my head

bowed, tears running down my cheeks. Because of Anita, her brother was learning to become compassionate.

However, when I told Leverett what the doctor reported, he said he wondered if the doctor wasn't right. He pointed out that Anita would get the kind of care in a children's home that she couldn't hope to get with us. "Besides," he pointed out, "she would always have a doctor close by."

I tried hard not to let Leverett see how my heart cried out at the thought of a "home." Once I visited such an institution that was run by the state, and I will never forget the filth on the walls and floors, and the wide-eyed children toddling around in rags. Of course, I realized that not all homes were that way, but I just could not let Anita go. Besides, every once in a while she would make a little advance that was cause for rejoicing.

I'll never forget one night when I was putting her to bed. I had taught her to place her hands together in prayer. Of course, she couldn't say anything, though I felt sure that she was communicating with her Father. That night she looked so fragile lying there, the lamp's soft light falling across her face. My heart filled and I hugged her and kissed her. Then, as I raised up, she looked at me so sweetly and said, "I love you, Mama." This was the first sentence she had ever said. I sank at her bedside giving thanks.

This breakthrough seemed to signal a new start for Anita. I found her standing at the window one day; she turned and said "Play . . . outside." I let her go out. And I'll never forget Bobby's running into the house, grabbing my dress, and shouting, "Look! Look!" He pointed out the window. Anita was slowly riding a tricycle.

But now our family had to make a new adjustment. Another child was coming. But instead of bringing joy, it only intensified Leverett's thoughtful conviction that

Anita be institutionalized. As he became really certain that it would be better for our family, and I just as adamantly refused, I told myself that no nurse could ever take the place of a mother.

However, as I lay awake at night wondering what was happening to Leverett and me, I realized that Anita was not the real cause of our growing estrangement. As I looked back on our wartime marriage, I could now see that I had come to it as a child. Neither of us had really known each other then and, as we matured through the years, we had grown further and further apart. By this time Leverett's mother had died, and I had lost a good friend. No, the disagreement between Leverett and me had only revealed the gulf that had widened between us.

Perhaps I was wrong. I must admit that our disagreement brought a lot of stress and anguish into our lives. The estrangement between Leverett and me intensified. Finally, it reached a point where we both agreed that a separation would be best.

For months I agonized. How had it all happened? Things like this were unthinkable in my family. And yet, by this time I realized—and I know that Leverett did too—that we had nothing in common. Our continuing to try to make our marriage work would only hurt each other and the children more. So, painful as it was to both of us, we reached the inevitable decision that a divorce was the best solution.

We parted on good terms and Leverett continued to contribute to the support of our children. Later, he remarried and moved to New Hampshire but continued to fulfill his responsibility to the children.

Now, I immersed myself even more deeply in my family and endeavored to become both father and mother to the children. On a beautiful June day in 1957, Teresa was born. She was a normal little girl. As I held her in my arms, I never realized the role she was destined to play in my life.

Teresa was perfect in every way. It was a good thing —for those were difficult days. For a time all the children stayed healthy. But then it seemed the material things would get bad. We had moved to a small stove-heated flat. In mid-winter we ran out of coal for the stove. In desperation, I went to a priest. For reasons I could not understand, he wouldn't help me. I broke up our chairs and burned them to keep us warm. There was a brief period when we ran completely out of money. For three nights in a row I went to bed without supper. Bobby was now ten, Anita was seven, and Teresa seven months. I worried about the children and wondered if getting married again wouldn't offer them the best security. After all, I was only twenty-nine. But would it be right for me to remarry?

The words seemed to come to me, gentle and low, "Have you not yet learned to trust Me fully?" The next Sunday morning in church I turned to the Lord: "O, Father," I prayed. "I know my responsibilities. And I know You will help me meet them as You promised. Father, I now pledge myself completely to You."

The next day a friend called. "Rita, we have three rooms for you in Waltham—a nice furnished place. Would you like to move?" As I hung up the phone, I felt God was already honoring my pledge.

Moreover, there was a lady in the building who was quite willing to stay with the children during the day so I could ask for work. I started out on an assembly line and seemed to have a mechanical aptitude. Within a few months I had become a quality-control inspector. The superintendent congratulated me; usually it takes a year's experience, he said, before someone is able to handle this task.

Now, I was able to get around more and visited friends I had made. During this time men often asked me for dates, and I found it easy to turn them down. But then one day a wealthy, handsome lawyer, whom I had come to know, asked to take me to New York for the weekend. I liked him very much and impulsively said yes. That night I couldn't sleep. I called the lawyer the next morning: "Bill, I'm sorry; I just can't do it." From then on, whenever temptation whispered, I would just silently pray to Him and He would always give me the strength to resist.

In the meantime, my sister, Enza, and her family had moved to the United States. I was so happy when they came over. We fell into each other's arms crying. And then wedding bells rang for the Settembres when my brother, Raphael, found the girl of his dreams in Italy. They married there and then came to Boston to live. That made quite a family of us here now: my sister, Enza, her husband, and their five boys; Raphael, his wife, and me. I wished that Mama and Federico would come but both preferred to stay in Naples. "It's my home," wrote Mama in a letter.

I needed the strength of a family close by in 1958. It happened on Teresa's first birthday. We had a little party for her. During the middle of it the phone rang. I picked it up, and the world turned black for me. Mama had died at home in Naples. We all knew that she had diabetes and high blood pressure. But I was not prepared. Mama died on the birthday of a grand-daughter she had never seen. I tried to keep my composure until the guests left. And then I broke down. All night I cried. Again I saw her as we said good-bye that last time in Florence. And from my heart surged the words of an old Italian song: "Mama, to you my song will fly. You'll never be alone for I love you so. These words of love that come from my heart . . . I'll always love you, Mama."

It took a long time for the ache in my heart to heal. And I was especially glad when my brother, Raphael, invited the children and me to live with his family. Raphael blossomed in America. Besides fathering twins, he developed great skill in decorating. In 1963 he purchased a house on Court Street in the Boston suburb of Brockton, and we all moved in.

All of us, except for Bobby. He was now sixteen and

becoming a man. A lively boy, he had inherited Leverett's mechanical skills, and was forever taking things apart and then reassembling them. I don't know how many times I found my kitchen chairs in pieces on the floor and then magically put back together, stronger than before. Bobby and his father often visited. However, I felt that a boy should really get to know his father and to benefit from the many things that only a father can help his son with. I discussed this with Leverett on the phone. He said he would be very happy for Bobby to come and live with his family.

Bobby looked forward to going. "But I'll be back to see you often, Mom," he said. "It's not very far." It really wasn't, for Leverett lived just up above the state line in New Hampshire. Bobby waved and walked off, then quickly turned and came back and kissed me. At sixteen he would still kiss me, even if he were only leaving for school. Once I jokingly referred to it and he said, "Well, Mom, you never know what can happen while I'm gone." Bobby did return often. And he did benefit much from being with his father. In 1965, when he was eighteen, Bobby volunteered for the U.S. Navy and served aboard the aircraft carrier *U.S.S. Wasp*. When he came to say good-bye, he pulled a book out of his pocket and showed it to me. "The Bible, Mom," he said. "It's going with me."

As our family dwindled, Raphael's family grew. Finally, he moved to a larger house, and Anita, Teresa, and I stayed at the little gray cottage on Court Street in Brockton, where we assumed the mortgage and the payments. It was here that so many events were shortly to take place, which were destined to change the course of history in our state.

It was a joyful occasion for everyone. For years I had prayed for a house of our own and again He had answered. In addition, I had to buy a car, for I was now driving fifty miles a day to the Sylvania plant in Needham to be at work by 7 A.M. In our area a car was a necessity.

One of the first things we did was to get a dog. The children had never been able to have one before. Lupo came to us as a lovable ball of fur who soon grew up to be a formidable-looking German shepherd. Even so, he was kind and gentle. But he was an excellent watchdog. He soon learned to recognize the steps of the mailman and milkman. But when a stranger came near the house, night or day, Lupo bristled. He *was* an excellent watchdog, but even so, he was kind and gentle with those he knew. He proved a close companion for Anita, especially on those days when I had to work. Leverett continued to help us, of course. But beyond our regular living expenses and the mortgage payments, there were Anita's medical and hospitalization bills. For by this time, she had had fourteen major operations in her sixteen years. Moreover, Teresa, now age ten, was going to school and needed books and clothes.

Throughout all this period I had the strongest sensation—without knowing why—that I was being, well—almost—*prepared* for something. Whenever the thought came to mind I tried to turn it aside with no success. Somehow Teresa was involved.

Even at her young age, Teresa, who was turning out to be a very self-reliant child, had become a real helper. When I got a job working evenings in a bridal shop, Teresa would come right home from school and begin making supper. She learned to prepare things like spaghetti sauce and lasagna better than I did.

In fact, it was I who was responsible for the major conflagration in our kitchen. To this day we call it "The Great Hamburger Fire." For supper one evening I had put some hamburger patties in the broiler oven. Then I got on the phone with a fellow member of an association to help retarded children. We had talked for some time, and suddenly I smelled something burning. The hamburgers! I rushed into the kitchen to see flames in the oven. I pulled open the oven door and ran for the phone to call the fire department. By now, thick smoke was billowing out of the kitchen. The firemen came, rushed into the kitchen, and soon came out wiping their eyes.

"What happened?" I asked excitedly. One of the firemen looked at me and shook his head. "Lady," he said, *"why* didn't you turn off the oven when the hamburgers began to burn?"

"You mean . . . the house isn't on fire?" I asked.

"No," he said, "but you've just burned up your dinner."

When the fumes finally cleared out we walked into a smoke-blackened kitchen. Everything—walls, ceiling, curtains—had been ruined. I told my insurance man about it, but instead of waiting for anything from the company, the girls and I spent a week cleaning up the mess. With walls scraped and repainted and new curtains, one could hardly tell what had happened. The only reminder was whenever I would be fixing hamburgers, Teresa would laugh, "Remember, Mom, no telephone calls!"

She was such a joyful child, always good humored, always sunny. She was the same way at her parochial school, according to her teachers. One of the priests at her school told me of an occasion when he overheard a group of girls talking about their fathers and all the things they did for them, taking them on trips and buying them gifts. One of the girls turned to Teresa and asked: "Where is your father? We have never seen him." Teresa smiled, and her dark eyes sparkled as she said, "I have my Heavenly Father. And He gives me *everything* I need."

I cried as he told me this, for many times I did not have this beautiful childlike faith. When I told the priest this, he said: "Remember, Rita, Jesus told us to come to Him as little children."

Complete faith, fully trusting faith was something I did not have. And the main fear that pursued me these years was worry over money. By the time our money came in, so much went immediately for necessities that sometimes I couldn't make our house payment.

Finally, I was seven months behind. The bank holding the mortgage had gone along with me for other missed periods, but one day the loan officer sorrowfully shook his head. "Mrs. Warren," he said, "we just can't go along with you any longer. You are four hundred and sixty dollars behind in payments."

I had until the coming Wednesday—three days away—to make the payment. Otherwise, the bank would be forced to foreclose.

On the Tuesday night before the deadline date, I went to bed knowing that I would have to lose our house. To go to Leverett was unthinkable. Even selling our old car would bring only fifty dollars or so. I twisted and turned. Where would we go? Raphael didn't have the room to take us in, and my sister, Enza, and her family had moved to California. Besides, I was too proud to ask them for money. As I lay there worrying, everyone else was asleep including Lupo, our German shepherd, who was snoring on the hall rug outside my bedroom. A cold fear of the future began to fill me and I started to sob. Choking and sniffling, I climbed out of bed and fell to my knees beside it, praying for help.

I don't know how long I knelt there, my head buried in my arms, when I heard a soft gentle voice calling: "Rita . . . Rita . . . everything will be all right." With a start I turned, and in the darkness of my room I thought I could hear someone coming toward me. I reached out and touched what felt like cloth. "Who's there!" I called in fright.

Teresa rushed into my room. "What happened, Mother?" she cried.

With the light turned on, I sat on my bed shaking. "Honey," I gasped, "I thought someone was in my room."

"But, Mother, how could that be?" she asked, brushing her long, black hair back from her face. "Lupo was sleeping outside your door." Lupo, still lying on the rug, the same dog who will jump and bristle when a stranger heads up the walk, acted now as if he hadn't heard a thing. However, now with the lights on and our talking, one eyelid opened as if he were wondering what all the fuss was about.

I touched Teresa's arm. "I'm sorry, Honey, I guess I'm just worried about the money we owe tomorrow."

"Mother," she soothed, "God said He would take care of things."

"Yes," I sobbed.

In ten-year-old simplicity, she said, "Mother, He promises to help us. We must trust Him."

She went back to bed. I turned off the light. As I lay there, my thoughts started to churn again. And then, a low light began to fill the room. It increased in intensity. And yet, strangely enough, I wasn't frightened. For that light carried with it the comforting touch of assurance. And now I knew who was in the room with me.

"Thank You, Jesus," I breathed. "Thank You for being with us."

The next morning with sunshine splashing through the windows, I sat at the breakfast table opening the mail. Among the bills and advertisements was a letter with my insurance company's address in the corner. "Oh-oh, another payment due," I thought. I slit open the envelope and drew out a letter along with a strange-colored slip of paper. I unfolded it and gasped.

The colored slip of paper was a settlement check from the insurance company for the smoke damages incurred in "The Big Hamburger Fire." It was for four hundred and sixty dollars, the exact amount we needed for our mortgage payments!

The fullness of His love flooded me with such an immensity that it seemed as if my very soul was floating up to Him.

As I sat at the table that morning looking out into the sunshine, I realized that there was only One in whom I could place my trust. I knew that no earthly leader, no society or government, or church authority, and—not even a husband—could take care of my family the way our Lord and Saviour, Jesus Christ, would. By this time I had gone far beyond considering myself a Roman Catholic or a Protestant. I was simply a follower of Jesus.

For I realized that our relationship with God must be a personal one, and therefore we do not need a middleman to reach our Heavenly Father. I respect the authority of the church, but I rest my faith on the personal presence of Jesus Christ as my Guide and Redeemer, and not on any man, ecclesiastical authority, ring, or symbol. For in speaking of the things of man, the Lord says, "Thou shalt not bow down thyself to them, nor serve them: for I the Lord thy God am a jealous God . . ." (Exodus 20:5).

Two years later, in November of 1969, as I lay in the hospital, stricken with pain, my mind searched back on all His assurances. I again heard Teresa's words, "But Mom, why can't someone with faith in God help bring prayer back to school?"

Now I knew in my heart that the same God who brought us through the terrible war, who kept Anita alive through fourteen major operations, who sustained our family, who even saved our house, would help me here, too. I knew now for certain that I must dedicate whatever time I had left in life to help put prayer back into school. I must do His will on earth.

4.

First Shots Fired

The sunlight trickled through the partially closed venetian blinds into my hospital room. I watched the shadow patterns on the ceiling, wavering and glimmering as the trees outside moved in the breeze. The sunlight, the rustling of the leaves, all spoke to me of God. It was quiet in the room. Father McCormick had been gone for several hours and I lay at peace now, listening to the murmur of voices in the hall.

There was a step at my door and my doctor walked into the room. He pulled a chair next to the bed and sat down. "Rita," he said, "we've found out what is causing you all that pain."

I looked at him expectantly—but no longer in fear. No matter what he would say, I now had Someone with me.

"X-rays show," he said, "that you have a stone in your gallbladder, much too large to pass. Normally, we would operate immediately," he continued, "but . . ." and he closed his notebook, his voice showing concern, "you are very weak, Rita. It would be dangerous to operate now."

I started to ask questions, but he continued, "What we'll do is build your resistance, keep you right here to give you a lot of rest and nourishment. Then we'll go into surgery."

Immediately I thought of Anita and Teresa, but then

realized that my brother, Raphael, and his family would take care of them.

"All right, doctor," was all I could say. Then I called Teresa and explained the situation. I was still surprised at the self-reliant way she accepted it at twelve years old.

"Okay, Mom," she said. "Remember to pray—Anita and I are praying for you." And then she asked in concern, "Do you have a Bible? I know you didn't take one in the rush. Yours is still right on the bedside table."

I smiled, "Yes, Honey, I have one. I pulled open the drawer of my little bedside table and there was a Bible right there. It was put there by the Gideons, that organization that puts Bibles in all the hotel and hospital rooms." I really was grateful. Without them, I would not have His Word to rest on. From time to time I would pick it up. I was too weak to read much, but just a passage or two each time was all I needed; they were either words of comfort or reassurance.

The next day I was wheeled down for more X-rays. I was shifted, turned and told to "be very still" many times as the giant machine scrutinized my body.

I awoke on the morning of my third day in the hospital to see the same sunlight shimmering on the ceiling. I knew that something strange had taken place— something that had directly affected me. A sense of deep joy seemed to fill the room, like an echo of an angel's song.

I lay there wondering. What was it? And the realization hit me suddenly—the pain was gone!

Completely, absolutely. I pressed my middle body, at first gingerly, then harder and harder. There was no question about it. The pain was gone.

"Thank You, Father," I breathed. Just then a nurse walked into the room. "Well, Mrs. Warren," she said in professional gaiety, "it looks like more X-rays for you this morning." Again I made that long journey down the halls, prone on the rolling cart.

That afternoon my doctor came in. But he did not sit down. Instead he paced back and forth at the foot of my bed looking at me quizzically. Finally, he said, "Rita, what did you do with it?"

"Do with what?"

He gave a brief laugh. "The stone. I can't understand it. It was too large to pass, you know. But today's X rays show no stone at all in your gall bladder." He walked out of the room shaking his head.

I reached for the phone and called Teresa.

"Honey," I said excitedly, "they can't find the stone."

She squealed in delight. "Mom, tell the doctor that God took it out."

Later that day my doctor said he was going to keep me in the hospital for more tests. "For at least two weeks, Rita," he said. "We want to find out what's going on."

They started feeding me spaghetti and meatballs and all the rich, spicy foods that would normally cause trouble for a person subject to gall bladder attacks. I ate thankfully with never a twinge.

It was work for them but fun for me. I was sitting up feeling completely well. In fact, I had never felt better in years.

One morning I picked up a women's magazine and started leafing through the pages—fashions, home decorating, party dishes. Suddenly it all seemed empty and meaningless. I put the magazine down. The room was still. Even the hall noises faded. It seemed as if time itself was waiting—and the dream I had the night before I became ill became very vivid. I had work to do, and I had better begin now.

To assemble some kind of a plan, I took some notepaper from the table, and began to jot down my thoughts.

A. *Goal?* To help make it possible for children to pray in their public schools again.

B. *Why?* Oppression begins by taking away small freedoms—the kind people wouldn't usually notice or talk about. Remember how the Fascist Party threw out all the history books except the one they approved? Hardly anyone really paid much attention to it. With small freedoms gone, then evil has an entrenched position from which to work on the foundations of society.

C. *How to Do It?* (But beside this question I put no notes.)

I lay there chewing on the end of my pencil for some time. How to start? I asked myself. *How do I start?*

I didn't know a thing about that Supreme Court school-prayer ruling, and all the complexities I was sure were involved. It all seemed so far away, so official, so involved with the higher-ups of government. I almost laughed at myself. Me, Rita Warren, a forty-one-year-old immigrant woman trying to change the law!

But something far deeper overrode these negative assumptions. I reached for my Bible on the bedside table and opened it: "Lo, I am with you alway . . ." (Matthew 28:20). The words seemed to glow on the page.

More and more in these past days I found myself reaching for the Bible. When all else failed, and I found myself groping for guidance, it was the one source of help of which I felt sure. And each time I turned to it in faith—fully expecting an answer—I always found one.

So, while the doctors puzzled over the mysterious disappearance of the gallstone, I lay back and wondered what He wanted me to do.

Where should I start?

Teresa's words came back to me: "Mother, if a woman without any faith was able to take prayer out of school, certainly a woman with faith can put prayer back in." I remembered how I had laughed and shrugged off this statement.

But now I wondered: Could *this apply to me? If so, where should I start?*

By getting some basic facts, I thought.

I didn't know much about the woman who had succeeded in the unbelievable feat of influencing the course of the government of the United States of America. Who was she?

I picked up the phone beside my bed and dialed Channel 7, a Boston television station. I had always watched their news. Maybe they could tell me. The girl in the studio was able to give me only her name and the town where she lived. Madalyn Murray O'Hair, Austin, Texas. She explained that at the time of the Supreme Court ruling in 1963, her name was just Madalyn Murray. But she had since married.

Madalyn Murray O'Hair—it began to come back to me. I vaguely remembered something about this woman, who called herself an Atheist, objecting to her son's reciting a prayer with his class in school. Somehow her complaint had reached the United States Supreme Court. And now, Teresa and thousands like her, were coming home with the words, "Mom, they won't let us pray in school."

What kind of a woman was this Madalyn Murray O'Hair? Certainly, she was a mother like me. But what made her think the way she did? How could one woman wield so much power—power to change something that had been accepted as part of our public life since the nation started?

Since the nation started. *Even before that,* I thought. I remembered a trip we had made once to Plymouth, Massachusetts, where the re-created *Mayflower* rests at her dock. As I stood in the lower cabin of this little ship I thrilled to think that I, too, had come to this country seeking a new life. I laughed, thinking that I probably suffered as much as the Pilgrims did aboard ship. And then the guide pointed out that it was here in this part of the ship that the people had written the Mayflower Compact as it rode at anchor off the shores of Massachusetts. I will never forget the opening words of that Compact: "In the Name of God, *Amen.*" Could those words be said in a public school today?

And still, today—one woman had changed so much. Who *is* she really? What is she like? As I sat in bed wondering about her, I came to a decision that was to be the first step in a succession of events that would affect my whole life. I decided to write to Madalyn Murray O'Hair. On some stationery Teresa brought me, I wrote Mrs. O'Hair that I wanted to meet her if she ever came to Boston. I wrote that I felt we should discuss the school-prayer situation. I was very polite, and wrote as one mother to another.

As the nurse walked out with my letter to post it, my doctor walked in. He brought happy news. I would be released from the hospital tomorrow!

"I still can't figure out what you did with it," he said, shaking his head. "All your tests show that you're in fine shape. There's nothing else I can do but to let you go."

"Doctor," I smiled, "I know what happened."

He looked at me, puzzled.

"God took it out."

He smiled in a bewildered sort of way, shook his head, wished me well, and never mentioned my diagnosis again.

It was a beautiful afternoon as I rode home from the hospital. The leaves were still flaming and in the late sun the trees cast long shadows across the road.

My country is such a beautiful place! I thought of the Pilgrims again, and of the Mayflower Compact, and of the Declaration of Independence, and the Constitution.

The Constitution. It struck me that I knew very little

about this most important document on which our country's laws were based. Something within me told me that this is where I would have to start.

Soon I was at the desk of our public library in Brockton. "What book do you have," I asked the lady, "that can tell me about our Constitution? I don't want anything complicated, but something simple that I can understand."

She puzzled for a moment, then went back to some shelves. She returned carrying a little red cloth-bound volume.

"This might help you," she said.

The book was called *The Faith of Our Fathers* by A. J. Cloud. A line at the bottom of the cover said: A HANDBOOK ON THE AMERICAN CONSTITUTION. I opened the cover. At the time of the writing in 1946, Mr. Cloud was President of the San Francisco Junior College in California.

That night I sat at our kitchen table studying the book. Teresa washed her hair, toweled it, and then sat across the table from me doing her homework. Anita was in her room watching television. Every so often I would have to ask Teresa to help me with a difficult word. I still couldn't read English too well.

"Mom," laughed Teresa, "by the time you're finished with that book, you'll do better in English than I do." And then she added with a chuckle, "I never thought you and I would be doing homework together."

I started reading the Preamble, that first part of the Constitution which begins: "We the people of the United States, in order to form a more perfect union . . ."

Mr. Cloud pointed out that this Preamble declares that the government of the United States was created to "secure the blessings of liberty by confirming the continuance among the people of those great personal rights and privileges pledged to free men in the Declaration of Independence."

As I read this I was again impressed by the wonderful freedom assured us. I shuddered, remembering my days in Naples during the war when the Nazis ordered us around at the point of a gun. And this freedom was not just reserved for the rich or high office-holders, Mr. Cloud pointed out, but "by the people as a whole —by the many, rather than by the few."

By the many, rather than the few. . . . I was stirred. And then I came to the First Amendment: "Congress shall make no law respecting an establishment of religion, or prohibiting the free exercise thereof; or abridging the freedom of speech, or of the press; or the right of the people peaceably to assemble, and to petition the Government for a redress of grievances."

The words: *no law prohibiting the free exercise of religion* burned before me. I read on, and the author explained that "Amendment I forbids Congress from establishing any religion—that is, setting up any state church—and from interfering with freedom of religious worship in any other respect."

My heart pounded. I looked up at Teresa bent over her books. Nobody wanted to set up a state church. All Teresa had asked to do was pray in school. And she was told that the government forbade this.

"Something doesn't make sense," I said aloud.

"You don't say!" said Teresa as she got up, closed her books, and yawned. "Neither does this algebra," she added. "I'm going to bed, Mom." She kissed me. "Good-night," and headed into her bedroom calling over her shoulder, "Keep studying like that, Mom, and you can become a lawyer."

For days I puzzled over the problems. The Constitution said one thing; Teresa was told another. I thought about writing the President of the United States but felt that wouldn't accomplish much. He has so much to do.

We continued reading *The Faith of Our Fathers*. In helping me with the big words, Teresa had also become interested in it. In his last chapter, which explains the basic principles of the Constitution, Mr. Cloud said, "Representative government rests on the will of the people as the ultimate sovereign—it is 'government of the people, by the people, for the people.'"

Suddenly it all came together. The majority rules. And certainly no one should infringe on the rights of the minority. But was it right for the minority to impose their will on the majority? What about government of the people, by the people, for the people? Couldn't the majority rule, and *still* respect the rights of those holding different views? This is the way I understood our government was set up from the information I received in the citizenship classes.

I talked to most of my neighbors and everyone agreed that the prayer ban was wrong. "But what can one do about it?" was the usual excuse. "What's done is done."

Well, I thought, *maybe if enough people made their feelings known, things might be changed.*

Just how many other people shared my feelings? I wondered. At first I thought about going from house to house to find out, but that wouldn't do. In the first place, I was working part time; but beyond that, it would take days to cover just my area of Brockton. And what would that prove? I needed to reach many people at once.

I sat on the living-room sofa and idly picked up the Brockton *Enterprise,* which Teresa had just brought in from the sidewalk. As I leafed through its pages I saw announcements from garden clubs, church socials, political meetings, and so forth. Then it struck me. *The newspaper!* Of course. This would be the way to reach nearly everyone.

The next morning I looked up the newspaper's address and drove over to its editorial office. I told the receptionist that I wanted to see the editor about a "very important subject."

Soon a girl came out into the reception room and led me into a large room. I had never been in a newspaper office before, and felt as if I were in a lion's den. All around me people worked busily at desks. Typewriters clattered and phones rang. I felt people were looking at me and wondering, "What's *she* doing here?"

Then I was standing before a gray-haired man sitting at a desk cluttered with papers. He was the editor. He looked up at me quizzically. "They tell me you have something of 'utmost importance.'" I got cold feet and wanted to walk right out. But he motioned me to sit down. "Tell me," he said, "what's on your mind." So I told him about my daughter's not being allowed to pray in school, and how I felt this went against our American heritage of freedom.

Yes, I knew all about the Supreme Court case, I said, in answer to his question, but pointed out that a lot of people I talked with felt it was wrong.

"And you want us to print a story giving your opinion?" he asked.

"Well," I said, feeling he might be looking for an excuse not to run the story, "I'm sure a lot of other people feel as I do."

He thought for a moment, then turned to me. "I'll tell you what I'll do. You bring me one thousand signatures of people who want prayer back in public schools and you'll get your story."

That afternoon Teresa and I were on the phone contacting our teenage friends and their parents. One of Teresa's friends had access to a mimeographing machine, and soon the petitions were being run off. Our kitchen table became the headquarters for the operation, and then it flooded over into the family room. An electric excitement filled all of us, and even Anita seemed to enjoy it as we gave her little jobs to do. For the first time, we had a concrete goal at which to aim.

Then, armed with petitions, we all took off in different directions. Scores of us stood in the street, in front of stores, in shopping centers—asking people to sign their names and addresses on a sheet headlined: WE THE UNDERSIGNED WISH TO RESTORE PRAYER IN PUBLIC SCHOOLS.

It was during the Christmas-shopping season and a New England winter was upon us. Youngsters shivered in the rain outside of office buildings and we mothers trudged door to door. We left petitions at churches for parishioners to fill out on Sunday.

As people signed their names, it was interesting to hear their comments. "Of course I want prayer back in school," said one man who then laughed, "but I don't think there's a chance of its ever happening."

Most people seemed to feel it was hopeless. After all, the highest court in the land had spoken. But they still wanted to put themselves on record as wanting it.

And then there were the few who called me "crazy." For as the word spread about what was going on at 898 Court Street, comments came back that some considered me a kook. "She's fighting windmills," said one acquaintance.

But no matter what they called me, we got our signatures. The Christmas season helped, for there were lots of shoppers on the street. Within two weeks we had more than a thousand names and addresses, and I proudly bore them to the editor.

The next day Teresa and I eagerly opened the *Enterprise*. There it was on page two: SCHOOL PRAYER DRIVE STARTED BY CITY WOMAN. "Mrs. Rita Warren of 898 Court Street has started a movement to bring prayer back to the public schools," read the first sentence. It went on to tell how the drive started, and then quoted me when I expressed my feelings that the power of God and His love was far stronger than man's power. "Without God there will be no country," I concluded.

I could hardly believe it. They were writing about me, a woman with only a fifth-grade education, who found it difficult to speak English. But then again, I knew that it was not me that brought this about. It was God.

While Teresa and I were discussing the story, the phone rang. Teresa ran for it, then turned to me, her eyes wide: "It's the Boston *Herald,* Mom," she said. The paper interviewed me over the phone, and the next day all of Boston read about our fight to bring prayer back into the public school.

People began to take notice, and a lot called to congratulate me. A Brockton lawyer who felt the same way I did, offered his services to the prayer campaign.

The day following the Boston newspaper story, the phone rang again. Teresa looked at me, holding the receiver, her brown eyes wider than ever. "Mom!" she whispered, "it's Channel 4!"

Channel 4 from Boston sent a television crew to our little gray house to film the story. That evening a crowd of teenaged prayer workers sat in the living room to watch the TV news.

After showing all of us, the commentator ended by saying, "Rita Warren, an immigrant from Italy, has a dream to restore school prayer. Will this miniature woman's dream achieve what seems to be an impossible task?"

A cheer rang up from the children and mothers sitting around me. I couldn't say anything. Tears flowed down my face.

But for some reason that night I began to have qualms, an uneasy feeling about it all. I looked around at our little group, just ordinary neighborhood young people. No college professors, no politicians, no one who knew the ins and outs of courts and legislation. Could we really *do* anything?

When you really got down to it, what did a few newspaper stories and television shows accomplish? Draw more ridicule from people who had already called me on the phone to tell me how foolish I was? Sud-

denly, I felt hopelessly inadequate. Maybe those who
called me crazy were right. I had enough to do without
getting involved in this prayer fight. Maybe I should
just retreat within my shell and forget it all.

And then one afternoon, Louis Angelo, a classmate
of Teresa's, was at our house. A tall, thin boy with a
shock of bushy hair, who spoke with a joyful voice, he
cared deeply for other people. Louis had been a big
help in getting petitions. Now, at fourteen, he had a
maturity far beyond his years.

"I'm so glad you are doing this for the kids," he said.

"Doing what?" I answered absentmindedly.

"Trying to bring prayer back to the school," he said.
He looked out the window, his eyes far away. "I'll
never forget back in 1963 when I was in public school
in the third grade. We used to say a little prayer each
morning. One day the teacher said that we couldn't
do that any more. All of us kids looked at each other
and asked, 'Why?' The teacher almost cried, and shook
her head, saying, 'I don't know. The authorities just
won't let us.'

"You know, Mrs. Warren," Louis continued, "there
were Protestant, Catholic, and Jewish kids in that
room. All of them wondered what was happening."

He picked up a cookie. "You're sure doing a good
thing," he said, "and we kids want to help you."

I stood looking at him for a long time. Then, not
able to hold back the tears, I took his hand. "Louis,"
I said, "God speaks out of the mouths of young people,
too."

Again, I reminded myself: with God all things are
possible.

That night I wondered about what I should do next.
A thought came. Take Teresa out of school to show
how I feel about her not being able to pray. Maybe
someone in charge will take notice. I explained this to
Teresa and she agreed.

So I officially took Teresa out of school. She stayed

home and I drove to her school and asked to see her principal. When they ushered me into his office, I was given strength to tell him that in good conscience I could not allow my daughter to attend school where there was no prayer. "I will see that she gets tutoring at home," I said.

He tried to talk me out of it, but my mind was made up. Then I drove over to the office of the school superintendent and gave the same explanation. A few days passed during which I had several discussions with both the principal and the school superintendent. Finally, I understood the superintendent to say that Teresa had permission to pray each morning between 7:30 and 7:35 A.M. in school, before classes officially opened.

Well, I thought, this was something. Teresa had a little prayer she had planned to give: "Dear God, give me the strength to learn, and grant us peace." But when I accompanied her to school, there evidently had been a misunderstanding, perhaps mine. For the principal met us at the door and said there had been no change in school policy. Teresa could not pray there.

Suddenly, the whole situation seemed ridiculous. It looked like praying in school was considered as dangerous as carrying a live bomb down the halls. I remembered a cartoon I had recently seen. It showed two little boys waiting outside their school principal's office. One turned to the other and said: "I got caught praying. What are you here for?"

I took Teresa home with me. I was determined that she would not return to school until she could freely exercise her conscience in prayer.

Now the school authorities warned me. Through neighbors the situation reached the newspapers. The school superintendent told reporters who questioned him about me that legal action may be taken against a mother who took her child out of school. Terming me in the Brockton *Enterprise* "a crusader," he explained in the newspaper account that "I am privately in sym-

pathy with prayer in the schools, but the Supreme
Court has ruled there shall be no prayer in school.
Mrs. Warren can keep her child out for seven days,
then we may be forced to take legal steps."

I began to worry so, that I became concerned that
the state would take Teresa away from me. "If that
happens," I promised, "I will send her on a plane back
to Italy." I wrote to President Nixon saying that if
such a thing happened, I would be the first American
citizen who left the United States because her child was
not allowed to pray in school. I was really concerned
by now.

President Nixon wrote back assuring me that it
would not be necessary for me to take such a drastic
step. Perhaps through Congress, he wrote, we could
achieve our goal to restore school prayer.

His letter cheered me and my concern subsided.
However, I didn't understand much about "Congress,"
except that it was a group of lawmakers who met regularly in Washington, D.C.

The thing that really inspired me at this time was a
large group of teenagers from the Brockton school.
They packed my living room one Friday night to discuss plans for a mass meeting we were planning to hold
in Brockton to gain public support of school prayer. We
had white and black children, kids from all faiths.

A reporter, Ralph Robbins, from the local newspaper attended and all of them let him know how they
felt about the issue. "They took prayer away from us
without even asking how we felt," said Louis Angelo.
"They say that Atheists might be offended because we
pray. Well, we're offended because we cannot pray."

"We are told that we are up against a stone wall,"
added fifteen-year-old Gail Welch. "Well," she declared, "stone walls have crumbled in the past. Look
at Jericho!"

William Cowan, another fifteen-year-old, said, "Our
forefathers came here looking for freedom of religion.

Well," he added mournfully, "that freedom might as well be taken out of the history books, because we don't have it anymore."

Stuart Glass, sixteen and Jewish, said that he favored school prayers, but pointed out that he felt it should be a universal prayer, one with which all faiths could agree. All of us quickly agreed that this is what we wanted, too.

In the meantime, we arranged for Teresa to be tutored by a local teacher. This way she was able to keep up with her classes. In the meantime, I continued working wherever I could at part-time jobs.

Because of the enthusiasm shown by so many students who wanted school prayer, our group felt that it would be good to have an open meeting of all the students to discuss the issue. To clear the meeting with the proper authorities, some mothers and I, along with Teresa and Anita, went to the office of our school superintendent. Some newspaper people, having heard about the meeting, accompanied us.

We asked to see the superintendent, but his secretary said that he was in conference. Perhaps I was becoming too sensitive at this point, but the idea that he was "in conference" grated against me. My temper began to rise.

"Then we'll wait for him if it takes all day and all night," I declared, sitting down on a couch. The others in my group joined me and silently waited as the secretary went about her duties. One of our group whispered to me that she had heard that the school had contacted the police. That didn't bother me but as we sat there, all the problems and worries of the past weeks seemed to build in me and my anger increased.

Then the superintendent walked into the room, and asked if we had an appointment. On learning that we did not, he said that he would be unable to meet with us. I struggled to keep my composure. Then, as we talked more, he said he'd grant us fifteen minutes. By now I wasn't thinking too clearly and I asked that the school committee be present also.

The superintendent turned to one of the ladies with me, and asked her to call him for an appointment. Then he turned and walked out of the room. Then, really losing my temper, I shouted, "You can't treat us this way!" At this point, a detective who had been called by the superintendent's office walked in and informed me that I was trespassing.

Hot with anger and convinced that I had a right to be in my child's school office as much as anybody, I refused to leave. At that, three detectives and two policemen walked in. One said, "Mrs. Warren, you are under arrest for trespassing and disturbing the peace."

What was happening! Each policeman took one of my arms and, walking beside me, urged me out of the office, down the steps and into the police car. I felt like I was a criminal. Anita and Teresa followed meekly, and got into the car, too. As they cowered beside me, we were driven to the police station.

Later, I was brought to trial before the judge. I stood there, hoping for justice. He looked down at me. "Mrs. Warren," he said, "I fine you three hundred dollars, and sentence you to two months in the Plymouth County House of Correction."

5.

We Do Our Homework

I couldn't believe it! Two months in jail and a three-hundred-dollar fine. The lighted courtroom globes seemed to swim before me. I stood looking up at the cold, impassive face of the judge.

My lawyer requested an appeal. Then he gently put his hand on my shoulder and drew me away. He led me into the outside corridor where I stood at the window. It had started raining since we had come in here, and now I watched it slant in gray sheets onto the streets.

Two months in jail. What would happen to the girls? Teresa was thirteen and Anita, though now twenty, still needed special care every day. Her doctor's words echoed from the past, "Mrs. Warren, the only thing that is keeping Anita alive is the love you give her every day."

Every day. Who would give her for two months the love she had been used to? Even my lawyer standing there, patting my shoulder didn't help.

But as I stood there, my mind going over past events, I knew in my heart that something of far deeper concern than man's punishment was troubling me. I knew that I was wrong in the superintendent's office. I was wrong in losing my temper. The Lord had told us very clearly: "Fear not, and be not dismayed at this great multitude; for the battle is not yours, but God's" (2 Chronicles 20:15 RSV).

In losing my temper, I had tried to take on the battle

myself. I looked out the window and prayed, "O, Lord, I can see that when I get angry I am trying to wage the battle instead of letting You handle it. Forgive me for not trusting in You."

A sense of calm came over me as I stood at the window—an assurance that everything would work out all right. Outside the rain began to stop. People who had ducked into doorways reappeared, and suddenly a patch of sun skipped along the street as a cloud rift scudded overhead. As I watched it, I felt a deep warmth inside, as if He was telling me, "Yes, Rita, you have many lessons to learn, but remember, through them I will be with you always . . . ."

"Rita . . . Rita." I awoke from my thoughts and turned. It was my lawyer. "Look," he said, "this isn't the end of the world. As you know, we're going to appeal to a higher court."

I was impressed by the fact that if a defendant is not satisfied with the judgment of his case, then he has every right to appeal to a superior court.

This was another revelation about the United States. So one could even argue with the court in this country! In a few weeks my lawyer and I appeared in the superior court. After my case was presented I was given the opportunity to plead guilty to trespassing and be dismissed, or declare my innocence and stand trial.

Again God's words came to me: "My battle, not yours."

"I lost my temper, Your Honor. I plead guilty to the charge."

I was given a lecture about propriety and then, my case was dismissed.

Right in the courtroom I thanked God. I also realized that I was learning more about our country's judicial system. By working within the law, one could achieve justice. Also I had gained a new appreciation of these men who have a knowledge of the law. I real-

ized how important a lawyer was to my prayer work. I
had gained a new realization of that lady holding the
scales of justice who was always shown blindfolded—
and those scales were not rigged!

As we walked down the courtroom steps into the
sunlight, I looked with new interest at the men and
women purposefully striding by. Many were lawyers,
I assumed, as they carried briefcases. But more domi-
nant in my mind was the realization that every dispute,
every controversy eventually came here. No matter
what the charges or arguments, the final decision was
decided in the courtroom. And each decision was based
on our laws.

An idea began to develop within me.

Obviously, school sit-ins, demonstrations, and fights
with authorities would not work in getting prayer back
into school.

But if we work through the law . . . ?

I began to get excited. The men who founded this
country had come up with a good set of rules by which
we lived. Over two hundred years of application had
proved those rules trustworthy. Why not work *within*
them to change the law?

A few nights later, Louis Angelo, the tall, thin high-
school senior, who had been with us from the start,
dropped over for a visit. I perceived a budding interest
in a government career in him, and he often came over
just to talk about the situation. As we sat around the
kitchen table, I brought up my idea of somehow, someway, changing the law.

"Well, Mom," said Teresa, her eyes sparkling, "I've
always said, that if one woman took prayer out of
school, couldn't another who believes in God be able
to put it back in?"

"And look at all the help you will get!" laughed
Louis, brushing back his unruly shock of black hair,
and glancing up at the ceiling. Then, he leaned forward

and in a serious tone, said: "You know, Mrs. Warren, I've always wondered what really happened back there in 1963. How did that one woman do it?"

Yes, how *did* she do it? I wondered to myself. Where were the Christians?

Again I thought of the library. I had found answers there before. The next morning found me at the desk where the lady had been so helpful. I asked for any books on the 1963 Supreme Court decision on school prayer. As she smiled and busily checked through her file, I marveled. What a blessing to walk into a library and get help like this without having to pay for it, or having to be someone important. I also chuckled to myself; this library lady must be wondering what the tiny woman with the foreign accent wanted with books on law and court decisions, when she normally would be taking out romantic novels or guides on home decorating.

In a little while I had an armload of books. The lady explained that they had no volumes on just the Supreme Court decision itself.

"School prayer has been a controversial subject over the years," she said, "and these books give an overall history of it."

"It all didn't start in 1963, then?"

"No," she smiled, "long, long before. But," she continued, "in these books you'll find information on the 1963 cases."

I drove home with the books and started going through them. Some of them I couldn't understand as they were so technical. Others seemed to be a little more clear to me; at least they had sections that even a fifth-grader like me could comprehend. But the library lady was right. There had been a long history of little known minor court skirmishes in various states involving school prayer or Bible reading. For example, in 1930, Joseph Lewis, President of the Freethinkers of America, tried to take the Bible out of the public

schools in New York. His aim was not successful—
then.

Nothing really important took place until those nine
justices in Washington rendered their decision. For all,
the lower courts tend to base their judgments on the
opinions handed down by the highest court in the land.

When the Supreme Court speaks, the nation listens.

But what about their famous decision in 1963? Here
I got a big surprise.

By now, Teresa was going through the books with
me. One evening she came to me, pointing to a page in
one of the books. "Mom, look!" she exclaimed.

I read the page she was pointing out. The famous
1963 school prayer decision seemed to stem from three
Supreme Court cases, one in 1962, and two in 1963.
The 1962 case banned the saying of a state-composed
prayer, and the 1963 cases outlawed the saying of the
Lord's Prayer and the devotional reading of the Bible.

The 1962 case resulted from a Federal suit instituted
by five parents of school children in New Hyde Park,
New York. They objected to their children saying a
state-composed prayer:

> Almighty God, we acknowledge our dependence
> upon Thee, and we beg Thy blessings upon us, our
> parents, our teachers and our country.

The Supreme Court ruled in the complaining parents'
favor, thus banning the saying of state-composed prayers in public schools throughout the nation.

Well, I thought to myself, in a sense I can understand
this. Lots of parents would not want their children
forced to repeat prayers that may not be in line with
their faith.

And then I came to the famous 1963 decision. It
was something of a revelation to me. For it was actually
based on two cases involving suits filed by two different

families: Mr. and Mrs. Edward Schempp of Abington, Pennsylvania, and Madalyn Murray (later Madalyn Murray O'Hair) and her son, William, of Baltimore, Maryland.

In the 1963 Schempp case, the parents protested a Pennsylvania law which called for the reading in class of at least ten verses from the Holy Bible at the opening of each public-school day.

Their children attended the Abington Senior-High School where devotions were broadcast into each classroom by students of the school's radio and television workshop. It was done under a teacher's supervision. The devotions included selections from the Bible, followed by the recitation of the Lord's Prayer, the flag salute, and pertinent announcements. Any child could be excused from class at this time if his parents so requested.

The Schempps, who were Unitarian, claimed that specific religious doctrines "purveyed by a literal reading of the Bible" were "contrary to the religious beliefs which they held and to their familial teaching." They decided against having their children excused from the devotions, feeling (among several reasons) that their children would be labeled as "odd balls."

And then we turned to the Madalyn Murray case. We read that her son, William, had been attending a Baltimore City public school which followed a Board of School Commissioners' ruling calling for the class to read aloud a chapter of the Holy Bible and/or the Lord's Prayer to begin each school day. Mrs. Murray and her son, both Atheists, had tried to have the school board rescind this rule but were unsuccessful. They then filed suit through the Supreme Court to stop this activity. I thought: another mother and child. How alike we were in one respect and so different in another!

In reading on, I learned that the court, in a joint decision, ruled in favor of the Schempps and Murrays, declaring that legally supported Bible reading was unconstitutional on the basis of church-state separation.

The court based its decision on the theory that the states involved were using their governmental powers in support of religion, thus violating the First Amendment.

I read this aloud to Teresa, who was going through these books with me after finishing her home-study school lessons. A local school-teacher friend was still coming in to tutor her daily.

Teresa looked puzzled after I read the statement about the First Amendment's being violated. "What do they mean?" she asked.

"Well," I said, "they mean the government should neither be for or against religion." I read her what Justice Tom Clark, who spoke for the Court's majority opinion said. Government action must have a "secular . . . purpose and a primary effect that neither advances or inhibits religion."

"Listen," I said. I turned to my *Faith of Our Fathers* book on the Constitution and read the first words of the First Amendment aloud to Teresa: "Congress shall make no law respecting an establishment of religion, or prohibiting the free exercise thereof . . . ."

I looked up. "You see? The Supreme Court meant that the government, in this case the states involved, had established a form of worship in the schools."

"Because the children had to repeat those prayers or read the Bible as devotions?" Teresa asked.

"Yes."

The room suddenly became silent. And as I sat there, I was conscious of an uneasy feeling building within me. To my own shock I found myself agreeing with much of what was being argued here regarding government influence. I had seen too many instances in other countries of how state religions became either ineffective puppets of government, or took on governmental authority, growing into power-hungry oppressors.

But then, as I continued reading the textbook, I got

a new insight. Not all of the Supreme Court justices agreed with the famous decision. Three of the nine justices dissented. One dissenter was Justice Potter Stewart. Though he agreed with part of the decision, he felt that the rights of those who want some religion introduced in the daily routine of the student had to be balanced against the rights of those who want their children entirely free from such influence.

He felt that to eliminate religious exercises from the public schools entirely was to place the first group at a disadvantage in order to grant the second group greater protection than their interests required.

As a result, Justice Stewart felt that the Court had established the religion of secularism—or at least the religious belief that devotional exercises should be conducted only in private. Thus, by absenting itself from the religious issue, the court was taking a stand for secularism.

Now the crux of the school prayer controversy became more clear to me. I could see that in guarding against one error, another far greater one may have been committed.

I read Justice Stewart's opinion aloud to Teresa.

She thought for a moment, looking up at the ceiling, then, brushing her long hair back from her eyes, turned back to me. "Mom, in the cases we read, were those kids forced to pray?"

"No, as far as I can see," I said. "Remember the Schempp children who were allowed to leave the classroom if they wished? I understand that if the children didn't want to take part in school devotions, they could be excused."

I yawned and looked at the clock. It was almost one o'clock in the morning. We had been studying the prayer situation for five hours.

Teresa got up, went to the cupboard for a cookie, and sat back down at the book-littered table. She bit into the cookie thoughtfully: "But Mom, we kids don't have to repeat any made-up prayer, or even read passages from the Bible. We could just make up our own prayers in our own words.

"Or," she continued, now sitting up, her eyes alight with a new idea, "even if they would just give us a minute to do it, we all could sit together and pray silently, each kid praying in the way he wants. If someone didn't want to pray, they could just sit there, thinking about their homework or something, and wouldn't have to feel funny or odd-ball about it."

At the moment, I didn't pay much attention to Teresa's statement. Not until later would I realize how prophetic it was.

Right now I was immersed in rereading the First Amendment: "Congress shall make no law respecting an establishment of religion, or *prohibiting the free exercise thereof . . . .*" Those last five words seemed to burn with fire.

True. The Supreme Court had declared that the recitation of the Lord's Prayer and the reading of Bible passages in the opening exercises of public schools were "religious ceremonies," and thus unconstitutional.

But what about that "prohibiting the free exercise thereof"? The Court seemed to be mainly concerned with *required* prayers and Bible readings, plus state-sponsored religious ceremonies. I saw nothing that would stop a person from praying on his own volition.

Moreover, as I continued reading the Court decision, I discovered a very interesting sidelight: the Court stated that study of the Bible or of religion was permissible "when presented objectively as part of a secular program of education!"

How many people knew this? I wondered. I grimaced as I remembered the high-school English teacher who was actually afraid to keep her own personal Bible in her desk in her classroom. "Because," she said, "Bibles are forbidden in school."

Suddenly, the immensity of what actually happened following the 1963 Supreme Court decision struck me. Where I had been fighting to stay awake, I now sat bolt upright in electric intensity.

Of course! Instead of studying what the Court really said, people jumped to the conclusion that *any* reference to prayer and the Bible in school was strictly forbidden!

I explained what I felt to Teresa.

"You don't say!" she giggled. "Like when Chicken Little said the sky was falling?"

"Almost," I laughed. "It certainly put a damper on talking about God or prayer in public schools."

"I'll say," said Teresa, "you should have seen the expression on my teacher's face when I first asked her about prayer." She laughed. "You would have thought I was asking permission to smoke at my desk."

I knew exactly what Teresa meant. My mind went back to other occasions. I remembered friends telling me in straightforward terms that "The government had absolutely forbidden prayer in public schools." And there was the mother from another school system who told me that her Parent Teachers Association's officers were afraid to open meetings with the nondenominational prayer printed in the PTA Handbook.

In effect, the free exercise of religion was being prohibited.

I remember when my former government would not allow us to read certain history books. As I went to bed that night, I thanked God that my children had escaped all that.

The next morning Teresa and I were back at the books. We could see through actual case histories how the Supreme Court ruling was interpreted in the years following that fateful decision.

For example, we read about Public School 184 of Whitestone, New York. There, the kindergartners, before having milk and cookies, used to give thanks: "God is great, God is good, and we thank Him for our food. *Amen.*" The principal, feeling this was illegal, put a stop to it. Upset parents, representing the Protestant, Roman Catholic, Jewish, and Armenian Apostolic faiths, fought for their children's right to give thanks. In a legal battle which dragged on for years, finally ending in a Federal court, they lost. The end ruling was decided on the basis that the teachers guided the children to say this prayer, and thus the children were not doing this of their own free will.

The court suggested that the school authorities might well permit those kindergartners who wish to pray to withdraw momentarily for this in another room; or, if this was not satisfactory, that they pass up their milk and cookies.

I tried to understand the court's thinking on this. Yet, I wondered if there wasn't some way we could avoid state-imposed prayer, but still allow free religious expression?

Meanwhile, Teresa was skipping ahead of me in her reading. "Oh, Mom," she groaned, "Look at *this* one."

The case she pointed out showed to what lengths opponents of school prayer will go when armed with the Supreme Court decision. And, also, how so much is open to interpretation.

To me, it highlighted our society's hypersensitivity to the prayer question, the nit-picking as to what was state imposed and what was not, and, in particular, the extremes to which our courts throughout the land had to go in order to determine whether something as innocent as a thank-you rhyme was lawful or not.

This case started in DeKalb, Illinois, which, I understand, is a farming and industrial community in the northern part of the state. A kindergarten teacher, Mrs. Esther Watne, had been leading the children in reciting the following lines each morning:

We thank You for the flowers so sweet;
We thank You for the food we eat;
We thank You for the birds that sing;
We thank You, God, for everything.

In 1964, the year following the Supreme Court decision, a local parent in that community complained to school authorities about this practice. Mrs. Esther Watne, the teacher, then deleted the word "God" from the last line of the verse so that it read: "We thank you for everything." This did not appease the parent.

This complaining parent was joined by the American Civil Liberties Union in 1966, in what became a long-standing battle. The school board refused to drop the verse, since they didn't feel the words constituted a prayer. The words *thank you,* they said, could refer to anyone, the milkman, the baker who made their cookies, or anyone on whom society depended.

At this, the parent filed a civil action in their local U.S. District Court. Theological professors and clergymen were called in to testify. They thought the words *did* constitute a prayer. However, the chief witness was the kindergarten teacher herself. The complaining parent's attorney pressed Mrs. Watne to admit that her verse was a subterfuge for prayer.

"No," said Mrs. Watne, who stated she regarded the verse as an expression of appreciation and gratitude for the whole world. She admitted that she did believe in God, but insisted that she hadn't presented the verse in a prayerful way.

The attorney then tried to get her to admit that children might sense her own devotional attitude—despite her efforts for religious neutrality.

She replied, "Well, I believe in a divine being, and I am thankful every day that I have a divine being who is guiding me. Now, if I bring that across to my classroom, I am not expressing it; that is my own philosophy, and I bring my philosophy into the classroom as a classroom teacher."

The attorney persisted in this line of questioning. "As a matter of fact," he said, "the thanks that you give when you have the children recite this little poem, and have recited for the past three years, is the thanks that you, as a human being who believes in a divine being, give for the wonders of nature, and which you hope to impart to your children, isn't that right?"

Answered Mrs. Watne, "Certainly. I tell them thanks for the trees and thanks for the flowers and thanks for all the food and everything that is in there. For them the whole world is open. Why shouldn't I tell them to thank Him?"

"Thank you," concluded the attorney. "No further questions."

By now I felt I was reading a Perry Mason case and I could hardly wait to get to the judge's decision. In rendering it, he said in part: "Despite the theologians' characterization of this verse as a prayer, the court believes that, set in the framework of the whole school day, its purpose was not to pray but to instill in the children an appreciation of and gratefulness for the world about them—the birds, the flowers, the food, and everything. . . . The defendant sought . . . to solve the complaint by deleting the reference to 'God'— nullifying any imputation of a prayer. . . . The court would be very reluctant to substitute its views as to how the aims of this kindergarten teacher to implant graciousness and gratitude in very young children should be accomplished."

And then came the judgment. The judge found in favor of the teacher. I mentally applauded—until I read further.

The attorney for the complaining parent filed an appeal. And, sad to say, the United States Court of Appeals for the Seventh Circuit reversed the previous decision, concluding that the offending verse "was the religious act of praising and thanking the Deity."

I sat there, my hands limply holding the book, and I marveled. Over three years battling in several courts, and thousands of dollars in expenditures, all to prevent little children from expressing gratefulness.

Where would it end?

Teresa was looking at a dollar which had been lying on the table to pay the paper boy. She handed it to me saying: "I wonder when they're going to change all the money?" I looked at the words on the bill: IN GOD WE TRUST. I smiled. It would be a big job. The same four words were on every coin we had. Yet, in my heart I knew there were many people who would fight to have those words removed, just as one parent fought to stop the kindergarten children in DeKalb, Illinois.

Where *would* it all end? I wondered. Would it reach the point of an official's stopping me from boarding a city bus some Sunday morning to ask where I was going? And when I would tell him "church" would he shake his head and inform me that I could not use the bus for religious purposes, since public transportation was subsidized by government funds?

As I was preparing supper that night, I wondered how Madalyn Murray O'Hair had done her work so well. I smiled to myself. Probably because she had the best publicity techniques.

I remembered that she was most recently in the news when she asked that the astronauts stop reading Bible Scripture from space. Thank God, that didn't go through. I wondered about this woman. In a way we had a strange relationship. She was a mother who, I had read, had taken her child out of school to protest school prayer. Here I had taken my child, Teresa, out of school because she couldn't pray. What caused Mrs. O'Hair to take this stand? Why had she become such a vehement fighter?

I was soon to find out.

In the meantime, Teresa and I continued to read everything we could get our hands on about the school-prayer controversy. Much of Teresa's time, of course, was spent in home study keeping up with her class-mates, but we still had time together to go over the material. And the school authorities weren't bothering us anymore, evidently because Teresa was being tutored.

I was concerned about Anita. I hadn't been spending as much time with her as I always had. But she seemed to take our busy-ness patiently, and contented herself with television. Then, I thought of giving her little jobs to do. One of these was to help me keep a file of news clippings. She would paste and help with the folders. These clippings showed that there were many other people involved in the same fight. From what I could tell, efforts to get prayer back into school settled down into these categories:

- *Test Cases.* A school in nearby Leyden, for example, was going ahead with a "moment of meditation" every morning to see what would happen.
- *Bills* to put prayer back in school on a national basis had been entered in Congress, but never seemed to get anywhere.
- *Praying Within the Law.* In the town of Netcong, New Jersey, for instance, the school board allowed children to assemble on a voluntary basis for five minutes before school started for a brief time of prayer. In an effort to keep it legal, one of the students read from the Congressional Record the prayer that was used to open Congress a few days previously. However, I read they were running into trouble. Later, the New Jersey Attorney General ruled it illegal on the basis of the First Amendment. The case finally reached the U.S. Supreme Court which found this unconstitutional.
- *Pro-prayer demonstrations* would flare up here and

there and then just as quickly die down, leaving no ripple.

- *Disregarding the law.* Many schools, I learned, completely ignored the historic court decision, and just went their own way, continuing to hold daily devotions. Many school superintendents, and even a few state governors, including George Wallace of Alabama and Ross Barnett of Mississippi, advised their teachers to continue with prayer and Bible reading.

The more I read, the more I saw a national dilemma. What was right and what was wrong? Some schools seemed almost overeager to keep the law, and others were pointedly ignoring it. I thought of the words of Abraham Lincoln before the Civil War: "And if a house is divided against itself, that house will not be able to stand" (Mark 3:25 RSV). It made me feel good to know that this great man read the Bible too. I wondered what he would have done in today's situation.

I somehow felt that he and I would agree. Children who wanted to pray in school—and couldn't—were being prohibited from their "free exercise of religion." Allowing them to say prayers would not be "establishing a religion," as long as no particular religion was being promoted, I reasoned.

The real dilemma, as I saw it, was how to preserve *both* freedoms: freedom from a state-dominated religion, and freedom to worship as one pleased.

I stepped into the living room and slumped down into a chair to think. How? I wondered. What was the answer?

I looked out the window far beyond the tree branches and low scudding clouds. "O Father," I prayed, "I'm not a lawyer or one experienced in state affairs. I need Your direction on this."

By now, I had learned the Lord answers our prayers in many ways. In this instance it was as if He took all the many things I had read on school prayer, and sorted them out in my mind in logical order.

"Voluntary prayer" kept coming to me. Develop one good school prayer law that would protect both freedoms—freedom from state control, and freedom of religious expression.

"Begin at home" was the other direction. Work through my own state's legislature. I could now see that I should start off by changing my state, not the whole nation at one sweep.

How this all would be accomplished was something He didn't choose to reveal to me at this time. But I did know that—in some unmistakable way—I would be directed by Him toward these goals.

Now I felt even more impelled to get this school-prayer message to the people. I did not have long to wait. A phone call came from a lady who said she was the secretary of the Brockton Grange Association. They wanted me to express my position at their next meeting.

Suddenly, while on the phone, the thought struck me. Answering questions on TV and radio was one thing, but giving a formal speech was another. I spoke English very poorly, and didn't feel I could talk that long without getting completely mixed up. I stammered to the woman that I would let them know.

After I hung up the phone, Teresa came out of the bathroom drying her hair. She had been shampooing her hair every day now. When I commented on it, she said, "cleanliness is next to Godliness." I put it down to another teen-age phase. As she toweled her hair, she looked at me sharply, "Mom, you're scared," she said.

"No, Teresa, you know me better than that." But I admitted I was wondering what I would say.

"Well, remember what you used to do? Whenever you had a question or a problem, you would go to the Bible and get the answer?"

Of course. Why? I wondered, as I went to get the Bible, *do we so often forget our obvious Source of help?*

I sat down with the Bible before me, praying for His direction, and opened the pages. No words flashed out at me; they rarely did. Instead, I continued reading. I was in Luke, chapter 12, and was reading about Christ addressing the multitudes when these words became very pertinent to me: "for the Holy Spirit will teach you in that very hour what you ought to say" (Luke 12:12 RSV).

Again, I felt Someone powerful standing close by my side.

There were about a hundred people in the Grange Hall that night. To me, standing up on the stage, my knees shaking, it seemed like thousands. I looked out on a sea of expectant faces. Inside, I silently prayed and words came: "Thank You, God," I said aloud, "to allow me to get as far with this struggle as You have." Then I began speaking to the audience. I called attention to the Ten Commandments, saying, "I am here to remind the Supreme Court that the first law we must obey is the law of God. He has taken an awful beating from the present adult generation of Americans, and it is up to us to put our country back to where she was at the beginning: 'Under God, with liberty and justice for all.' "

That speech was a start. From then on invitations flowed in for me to speak at churches, civic groups, and local television programs.

Louis Angelo, bless his soul, was busy, too. Louis's burning interest in the prayer issue, which he so well expressed at my house, led him to start speaking in churches around the area. The earnest spirit of this boy with the ringing voice seemed to touch people, and he also became more and more articulate. I particularly remember the night he told me he was speaking before the Pentecost United Methodist Church. I marveled.

Here was a Roman Catholic boy speaking to a Protestant church. In fact, it was the Protestant churches in our area that really got behind our movement from the start.

Teresa did her part by writing letters to the editors of local newspapers. One of her best efforts read: "Many people think that we are fighting for just prayer in school, but we are fighting for principles. I feel that it is my privilege to pray and respect God where I want, when I want, and in what way I want." It was printed in our local paper and I never saw an author any prouder. I was so proud of her I held myself back from commenting on the fact that I wouldn't recognize her anymore without a towel around her hair.

An increasing number of invitations for me to speak came through the mail and over the phone. These included requests from local colleges and educational associations. I tried to satisfy everybody. But one thought kept bothering me. We still were not reaching the nation. The Boston area was one thing but what about all those parents whose children were not allowed to pray in school in California? Florida? Illinois?

This concern grew within me, and one night I prayed: "O Lord, how can we let the people in other states know about this?" The next day an attractive young woman was at my door. She said her name was Marlene Sanders and was from ABC News in New York City. I invited her in, and along with her trouped in several men with lights. She interviewed me right in my living room, and I hoped the cameras would pick up the picture of Jesus I have on the wall.

The next day my story was on nationwide news. The picture of Jesus didn't show, but my story must have touched the hearts of a lot of people. The mail really started pouring in. To be sure, we had previously received letters from local people, praising me for my stand, or condemning me. But now that the nation knew, the letters began to pile up on our kitchen table so high that Teresa and I couldn't see each other if we stood on opposite sides of it.

Between her tutored lessons and school work (and shampooing her hair), Teresa tried to answer the letters on our little broken-down typewriter. One afternoon, after working all day on letters, she looked up at me and brushing her long hair back from her eyes she laughed: "Mom, sometimes I wish I had never come home that day and told you they wouldn't let us pray in school!"

Anita was a big help folding letters and stuffing envelopes. What she lacked in speed she made up for with patience. Often I would watch her as she worked slowly and laboriously folding a letter with her poor little misshapened hands, but always doing it carefully and neatly. *Dear, dear Anita,* I thought to myself, *what she may be missing in physical skills and facilities had been more than made up for by the spiritual peace and joy our Lord had given her.*

Many of the teenagers who had circulated the petitions also came over and helped. Oftentimes it was like a big party going on in our house, with everybody laughing and talking while they worked.

We all were inspired by the letters. In fact, on some nights, long after the last helper had left, and Teresa and Anita were asleep, I would look at the stacks of letters and feel a warm glow. It was as if they were saying: "Look, don't let down . . . there are thousands of us all over the United States who are with you."

Some of the letters were poignant. I still treasure one from an American G.I., Sgt. Steve Johnson, who wrote from Viet Nam:

I'm so happy to see that someone in the world back home is concerned with issues that are important. I get so tired reading about messed-up people . . . and trash news. America is doomed like Sodom and Gomorrah unless it realizes there is a God who will only take so much sin. He will forgive, however, and I pray every night that He will spare America. My letter is short, but my prayers are long.

Later I learned that this young man had been killed in action. I wondered if this was his last letter. What a message to the American people. Even the letters from some of our opponents seemed favorable. Many seemed to be torn by conflicting loyalties, aware of the blessings of school prayer on one side, yet bound by a legalistic interpretation of the law on the other. Such a one, I felt, was our state's Attorney General, who had acted against our neighboring town of Leyden which had tried having prayer in school before classes started. He wrote to assure me that his action was completely non-partisan. He also praised me for my interest and effort as a public-spirited citizen.

And then came the phone call I will never forget. It was from a man representing the Ed Miller television show "Speak Out" on Boston's Channel 7. "Would you like to debate Mrs. Madalyn Murray O'Hair on television?"

Before my common sense could take over, I gulped, "Yes."

After hanging up the phone, I really wondered what I had walked into. I knew that this woman was a highly educated woman—a lawyer, in fact. The more people with whom I discussed my impending debate, the more concerned I became. Some people warned me not to go near her. "She's a maniac. She'll tear you to pieces. You'll look like a fool in front of all those people."

One Catholic priest traveled all the way from Washington, D.C., to convince me to back out of the debate. "She is the devil himself," he warned.

But I had committed myself. Finally, the day for the debate arrived. I took Teresa and Anita with me to the studio. At first, I used to worry about taking the girls with me so many places. But they seemed to enjoy it; even Anita would later make brief comments about the people she met.

The staff welcomed me warmly. "Mrs. O'Hair is already here," they said. "She's waiting in the studio. Come in and meet her."

Praying fervently in my heart, I patted Anita and Teresa on the shoulder, and then, taking a deep breath, followed my escort to the studio door. On the other side of it waited the much-publicized Atheist, who stopped more people from praying than all the pagan Roman emperors put together.

I said a prayer to Jesus and walked through the door.

6.

Meeting Madalyn Murray O'Hair

I recognized her immediately. Not that I had seen her before, but there was something unmistakably fortresslike about the substantially built woman who sat quietly in the chair. I was reminded of a battleship at anchor. Her cool gray eyes searched me as I walked across the studio toward her. They looked out from a broad, pleasant face, framed by close-cropped white hair. But the jaw gave her away. It was a granite cliff. The crinkly laugh lines around her eyes did not lessen the apprehension within me. Something warned me: "Watch out for her humor; it's deadly. She will nail you to the wall with a quip."

But as I continued toward her, praying as I walked, a strange thing happened. A flood of compassion for this woman filled my heart. I did not see an enemy, only another human being.

I reached out my hand to her and said: "Hi, you must be Madalyn O'Hair." She rose from her chair.

"Yes," she answered, smiling, "and you must be Rita Warren."

We sat down in the adjoining chairs they had placed for us, and for a moment, I wasn't sure of what next to say. Then, in the most natural way as any mother, I turned to her: "How many children do you have?"

"Two," she said, and then her eyes sparkled, "plus a little granddaughter. I love her! And how many do you have?" she asked.

I told her about Bobby, Anita, and Teresa and suddenly all barriers were down as we sat chatting like any two mothers over a back fence. "You know, Madalyn," I said, calling her by her first name quite naturally, "I think we are going to become friends."

"Friendly enemies, perhaps," she smiled.

"No, Madalyn," I laughed. "Love makes friends, not enemies."

We had little more opportunity to talk. The announcer wanted to seat us because the show was about to begin. Suddenly, before I realized it, Madalyn Murray O'Hair and I were sitting across from each other under the hot studio lights. In the glare I couldn't see Anita and Teresa, who sat out in the audience. Then we were given the signal and thousands of people in the Boston area were watching us.

I remember little about that debate. All we really proved, I think, was that each of us held strong convictions. The one thing that impressed me most was that through it all I did not feel any animosity toward Madalyn, nor did I sense any from her. Our debate was hot but friendly.

Finally, it was over. Both of us sighed, got up and stepped toward each other laughing in relief. The announcer congratulated us and said that it was "a draw."

Again, we began chatting like new neighbors who had just met. Anita and Teresa came in from the audience area, and I introduced them to Madalyn. There is something telling about the way an adult responds to a disfigured, retarded person. And Madalyn hugged Anita close to her. As we talked about our children, a flash of deep concern crossed Madalyn's face. She quietly mentioned that her older son, Bill, aged twenty-three, the one in the Supreme Court case, had left home and no one knew where he was. She added in an almost imperceptible voice, "I'm afraid he may be dead."

Impulsively, as I would for any worried mother, I blurted, "Oh, Madalyn, I will pray for Bill that he will return home safely." I wondered to myself: Was all the notoriety through the years too much for Bill? Is that why he ran away?

She looked at me, smiled quickly, and started talking about her younger son Garth, now fifteen, just about Teresa's age, and her five-year-old granddaughter Robin, who was Bill's child.

Our conversation had to end as we had both agreed to appear on another talk show that same night: Channel 38's "Cracker Barrel" with Tom Larson. We moved on to another studio, met the producer, Donna Grant, and again sat before the cameras, each making our own points, and attacking the other's arguments with what we hoped was devastating effectiveness.

I do especially remember making a point on how I believe faith moves mountains, and I called attention to Anita's miraculous recovery from many illnesses as proof. "And I feel in my heart," I added, looking at Madalyn, "that this same faith can bring prayer back into the schools."

By now I had become accustomed to the television studio atmosphere, the glassy eye of the camera, the director hovering offscreen. In fact, I was getting to like it! In a short time, I had achieved a confidence in debating that I had never dreamed of possessing. I appreciated that instead of attacking each other personally, Madalyn and I concentrated on each other's position. Sometimes she would catch me off balance; at other times I would take great relish in neatly puncturing an argument she was ballooning. Again, at the end of the program, we were told it was a draw.

"Well," I said, stretching. "All's well that ends well."

"But there will be another time," Madalyn laughed. She reached into a large bag she carried with her and brought out a book. "Here," she said, her gray eyes sparkling, "maybe I can educate you." She wrote something inside its cover and handed the volume to me. It was her autobiography: *What on Earth Is an Atheist?*

I opened the cover and on the flyleaf read: FOR RITA WARREN—KEEP UP THE FIGHT! MADALYN MURRAY O'HAIR.

I was deeply touched. "Thank you, Madalyn," I said, wishing that I had something to give her in return.

Madalyn said she had to catch a plane. We said our goodbyes, she gave Teresa and Anita a hug, and was out the door.

I stood in a daze. I had come expecting a bitter fight with an ogre who (I had been warned) was an agent of evil. Instead, I had met another mother, an intelligent, sensitive woman who seemed deeply human. I could not accept her convictions. But I could love her as a child of God. I felt sure that He had arranged for us to meet, and I hoped that we would meet again some day.

I turned, gathered my girls together, and we drove to our little house on Court Street. When we arrived home, the first thing the three of us did was to hold hands and pray for the safe return of Madalyn's son, Bill.

Gradually, "The Great Debate," as Teresa called it, faded from our minds.

For a time, nothing seemed to be happening in our school-prayer campaign. It was a lull period, and I suppose I should have recognized it as such. But in my impatience, I began to feel blue and depressed.

One evening, while reading a news magazine, I noticed a reference to the various groups headquartered in Washington, D.C., which advocated a new amendment to the Constitution in favor of school prayer.

Suddenly it struck me. Wasn't it time for us to visit these people? Compare notes? Find out what they were doing on a national basis? I also had to admit I was hungry for fellowship with others who felt as I did about school prayer. Teresa also thought it a great idea.

"But how will we get there?" I brooded aloud. "We have hardly enough gas money to drive to Boston, much less Washington."

"Oh, Mom," chided Teresa. "Look who doesn't have the faith now. Why don't we do like you always say? Pray about it."

So, together, the three of us, Teresa, Anita, and I sat and asked the Lord to show us the way to Washington.

The first thing He did was show us that it wouldn't be just the three of us, but a number of the young people who had helped out before. And then came the date. February 15. It was a natural; the youngsters had that week off as a school vacation, and I was able to get away from my job.

In the meantime, some surprising things happened. One morning we found a thick manila envelope in the mail with no return address. I opened it to find currency with a brief note requesting that it be used in our "work." I was flabbergasted.

But Teresa was already on the phone calling a rental car agency. A rental car? "What do we need with a rental car?" I called. "Mom," said Teresa, after hanging up. "First of all, we'll need a station wagon; that old thing of ours won't take all those kids. And in the second place, I bet our car wouldn't even get us to Route 128."

So, on the morning of St. Valentine's Day 1970, our little group started loading up the rented station wagon. Tall Louis Angelo and chunky Everett Hayward, both high-school seniors, made a good pair in securing a good part of the luggage on top of the wagon. The girls, Gail Welch, a red-haired sophomore; Michelle Elsmore, a senior; Linda Nota, a junior, who helped Teresa keep up with her classes; and Teresa and Anita, all giggling and talking, made sandwiches and filled thermos bottles. It would be a long trip, and we had no money to stop at restaurants along the way.

Finally, we all crawled in and the station wagon looked like an elephant as we lumbered away from Court Street. The last that Boston saw of us as we slipped on to the Turnpike was a big sign in our back window:

DON'T GROW UP TO BE A FOOL
HELP BRING PRAYER BACK TO SCHOOL

As we rolled along we talked about the people we were going to see. Through the help of my local representative, we had appointments with several congressmen. While in Washington we planned to stay with Mrs. Laura Miller who coordinated the work of a movement called "Back to God." We also hoped to visit Father Robert Howes, national director of another prayer-in-school movement. It sounded like a busy stay.

Late that evening, we drove into the capital. There it was: the Washington Monument! All lighted, the beautiful spire reminded me of a church steeple pointing to God. My breath caught as we passed so many buildings I had long heard about, even as a child in Italy. I had a strange feeling as we looked at the United States Supreme Court building where ironically this trip really started. I smiled, remembering that the clerk opens each session with the words, "God save this honorable Court."

Mrs. Miller turned out to be just as warm and charming as her letters. "Come in! Snacks are ready!" she greeted us, her dark eyes shining. As we ate, we talked nonstop. She told us about the work she and her friends were doing to bring about an amendment to the Constitution that would allow prayer in schools. "Odd, isn't it," Mrs. Miller said, "how we will pay a chaplain $33,000 a year to lead Congress in prayer each day, but find it illegal to open our school day with prayer!"

Odd indeed. We were anxious to meet some of these Congressmen. Early Monday morning we headed for Capitol Hill, where we found a wide variety of opinion about our mission. Of course there were some who were opposed to what we were doing, like the Representative who let me know that he was a "big man in Washington." He ridiculed the idea of a prayer amend-

ment, and said we didn't have a chance. Then there
were those who obviously did not care one way or the
other. "My children pray in parochial school," said one
man quite bluntly. "Why should I worry about kids in
public schools?"

But such were in the minority. We met many, many
Congressmen and Senators who favored a prayer bill.
I'll never forget the first time we had a Congressman
paged from the floor to learn his feelings on the subject.

"Mom," whispered Teresa, "how can you do something like that? He is an important man."

"Sure he is, Honey. But don't forget we are important, too. We are American citizens, and these men
work for us. We have every right to find out their
opinions."

In no case did we find any of these men disturbed by
our questions. On the contrary, they seemed to welcome our interest.

One of the people we met was Emanuel Celler, a
Representative from New York, who was chairman of
the House Judiciary Committee. Mr. Celler said that
some 110 prayer bills were currently pending before
the committee. "But remember," he said, "Congress in
the past has not been able to agree on a prayer bill.
But—if enough support could be shown, there might be
some hope."

Undoubtedly, however, the highlight of our visit to
the men on Capitol Hill came when we went to see
Mr. John McCormack, the Speaker of the House who
is from Massachusetts. I knew that Mr. McCormack
had served under eight presidents, and helped to make
some of the most momentous decisions a country has
ever had to face. His career spanned an era from the
time when the coal-burning battleships of our "great
white fleet" traveled around the world to when our
space rockets landed United States astronauts on the

moon. I had followed his career for years in the newspapers, and so I was somewhat breathless as the secretary ushered us into his office.

As we walked in, the tall, slim, distinguished-looking man rose from his chair behind a desk. In the light from a tall window, his white hair shone like silver. I stepped forward and took his outstretched hand.

He smiled and said: "Are you the little woman who is making all the trouble in Massachusetts?"

The fear within me melted and I relaxed. "It's good trouble," I laughed, "not bad trouble."

He told me that if he was still a member of the House of Representatives when the prayer bill came before it, he would vote for it. He chuckled and told me the story of how, in 1963, the words IN GOD WE TRUST were placed above the Speaker's rostrum in the House of Representatives.

"Previously, there were just several engraved stars occupying that space," he said. "To me, they had no historical significance. But, I thought, what would be more meaningful than to replace them with our country's motto?"

Mr. McCormack said this had happened shortly after the Supreme Court decision banning school prayer. "But the timing was purely coincidental," he said. I thought I detected a trace of a faint smile on his face.

"God be with you in your work," he said, as we parted. I thought, as we walked out into the hall, that if our trip had resulted in nothing more than our seeing Mr. McCormack, it all would have been worth it. "God be with you in your work," he had said.

With men like this on our side, I wondered why it was that so many bills came up in Congress supporting prayer in school, yet nothing happened. I got one answer from a visit with Father Robert Howes, so active in the put-prayer-back-in-school campaign. He congratulated our little group on its work in Massachusetts.

"But you know," he said, "all of us in this fight are

facing a strange phenomenon. Lawmakers tend to listen to big-name religious leaders. Poll after poll indicates that more than 80 percent of grass-roots America support free-school prayer with only some 12 percent in opposition. The big-name leaders who oppose a carefully worded prayer bill obviously do not speak for their own people. We call them 'Generals Without Armies.' "

The more I talked with these men and women, the more a thought kept nudging me.

I had met a lot of people in Washington like Mrs. Miller, Father Howes, Senators, Representatives, and other government officials who were diligently working for a constitutional school-prayer amendment.

But who was working for school prayer back in my own state capital? More and more I was getting the impression that *my* work should start at home—back in Massachusetts.

So our trip drew to a close with a far clearer objective. Most important, too, we no longer felt so alone. We knew now that there were others all over the country working for the same cause. We headed home with a new charge of energy, determined to move every mountain blocking school prayer.

As we neared Boston late that night, we could see the lighted towers where our country's fight for liberty began. Now, in this same city we would begin another fight. For as we drove over streets that patriots had walked two hundred years ago, I vowed that I would employ every legal means, as an American citizen, to put prayer back into the public schools of Massachusetts.

To accomplish this I would become involved in something I wouldn't even have dreamed of a year ago. I decided that it was time to file a bill on the behalf of school prayer in our state's Legislature.

7.

The Battle on Beacon Hill

How does an ordinary citizen go about changing a law?

A year ago such a question would be as unthinkable to me as designing a space rocket. Also, a few years ago I labored under the Old World thought that common people should tend their gardens; only high leaders had the intelligence required to govern a country. Of course, when Mussolini and his "eternal regime" collapsed, so did the idea that these important leaders had any special governing rights. In America, though, people were supposed to run their own country.

But even in America I noticed that a lot of people paid little attention to their government, except at election time—when candidates sought their favor. Then, under the barrage of handbills, door-to-door visits, and television campaigning, politics became a big thing, like the World Series baseball games. But after the candidates were settled in office, thoughts of the voters seemed to revert back to home and garden.

Lately, however, I noticed that more and more people were becoming concerned with their government, particularly the younger folks. That seemed good to me. Perhaps Madalyn Murray O'Hair did a good thing when she got legislation against school prayer. This may have been one of the things that stirred people up enough to get concerned with their government.

It certainly stirred me up. So, realizing that sit-ins,

newspaper stories, speeches, and demonstrations were —in the end—ineffective, I decided to try to enact legislation to put prayer back into school by working within our democratic system.

The Massachusetts State House is on Beacon Hill in Boston, and it all starts here. A beautiful, ancient building with a resplendent gold dome, tourists come here to see the famous wooden codfish hanging in the House of Representative chambers which symbolizes our state's fishing industry.

But on that bright late winter morning I went there with business on my mind. Before climbing the wide steps, I stood for a moment looking at the statues which dot its landscaped grounds. Two of them were women; one was Anne Hutchinson, who was banished from the Colony in the early seventeenth century because she dared to question the narrow Puritan theology; and the other was Mary Dyer, who was a martyr for her Quaker faith. I hoped that those hallowed ladies weren't trying to tell me something!

No matter what, I couldn't turn back now. In Massachusetts, as in other states, any citizen has the privilege of filing a bill. It must be filed through a State Representative. I had phoned Representative George Young for an appointment. He was not from my district, but that didn't matter. For a bill can be filed through any Representative. I chose George Young because I knew that he was in favor of such a bill.

I also knew that Representatives are lawfully bound to file a bill upon a citizen's request even if the Representative does not agree with it. However, I felt it best to begin with someone who felt as strongly in favor of the projected bill as I.

I had arrived about fifteen minutes early for the appointment. I took this opportunity to climb the stairs to the visitor's gallery of the House of Representatives. This is where it would all begin, and I wanted to sit here for a moment. The House was not in session, and as I sat down behind the carved walnut railing of the gallery, the lights were dim, and a few cleaning people worked among the semicircles of desks on the floor. At these desks sat the two hundred and forty men and women who represent the nearly six million people of Massachusetts in the one hundred and seventy districts making up our commonwealth.

Above me hung the famous sacred cod, and before me on the walls behind the speaker's platform hung large oil paintings depicting historical high points in the growth of freedom in Massachusetts, from the Pilgrims' landing to John Hancock's asking that the Bill of Rights be included in the Federal Constitution.

As I sat there, I found myself gripping the rail, and a chill creeping over me. Who was I to become involved in all the complicated legislative process that would take place on this floor?

I shut my eyes and quietly prayed for God's blessing and guidance. If I wasn't supposed to do this, well, then I felt that George Young would tell me something that would make me realize this. If I was, in some way I would get the feeling to go ahead.

I opened my eyes, and as I continued looking over the hushed chamber, I noticed the large electronic voting board to the left of the speaker's podium. I had heard about this tally board. It bears the name of each of the 240 representatives with a red and a green light bulb next to the individual's name. When a vote is called, each representative presses a *yes* or *no* button on his desk and the appropriate bulb lights up. Thus the decision is easy to see almost immediately. Green for *yes*. Red for *no*. As I sat there I wondered: How many green lights would flash in favor of the school-prayer bill?

I glanced at my watch; it was almost time for my appointment. I walked downstairs and found the glass door of George Young. A secretary ushered me in, and he greeted me warmly.

He was a distinguished-looking man with kind, understanding eyes. After drawing up a chair for me to sit down, he leaned back and listened attentively as I explained my mission. Somehow, his very interest gave me confidence. When I finished, he said yes, he would be very happy to file a bill for legislation to allow prayer in the public schools.

"Does it cost anything?" I asked, knowing well the condition of my personal finances.

"No," he smiled, "just your time if you really want to see it through.

"I mean that," he added. "Just putting a bill into the works is no guarantee that it will get anywhere. It immediately becomes fair game for anyone who wants to knock it down. You will have to fight for it, Mrs. Warren, push it, prod it." He looked at me seriously: "Okay?"

"Okay!"

"All right," he said. "I will have it written up for you."

He explained that he would file a petition for legislation in the office of the Clerk of the House of Representatives. A lawyer from the state would write it up in a form that would be phrased correctly from a legal standpoint, he said. Then I would have to approve it, and sign it.

"When will it be ready for me to sign?"

"Give it about three weeks; I'll let you know, Mrs. Warren." He escorted me to his office door, and as we parted, we shook hands. "Don't worry," he said, "I'm on your side."

While I waited, I wondered what would happen next. I had a vague idea of the bill going to the House and Senate, but actually what really happened to it was something I knew little about. I went to Mary Fantasia, a Representative from the Somerville District. I had known her for some time and often looked to her for advice. A vivacious woman, her blue eyes sparkled with interest as I told her about my plans. She was all for the bill.

As we sat in her comfortable office over coffee, I asked, "Mary, what will happen to that bill after I sign it?"

"It will go through the regular legislative process," she said. "First the Clerk will give it a House number and assign it to a joint committee for discussion. Most of these committees are made up of six Senators and fifteen Representatives with both a Senate and House chairman.

"Your bill will go to the Education Committee," she said. "They will give it a public hearing and then, after discussing it, will pass it on to the House with a recommendation of 'pass' or 'ought not to pass.' "

"Does 'ought not to pass' mean it's dead?"

"Usually," she said. "But there is also the danger of the bill's never getting out of the committee when the members can't agree on it pro or con," she added. "This is when it 'dies' in the committee."

I swallowed. "What's the next hurdle, Mary?"

"With a favorable report from the committee, it will go to the House for debate."

"And if it is passed?"

In answer she picked up a State House pamphlet and handed it to me, pointing out explanatory paragraphs: If approved, the bill goes to the Senate. When both the House and Senate have passed the bill in exactly the same form, it is then printed for final passage and returns for the vote of enactment. If the bill is changed by amendments in one house, it must return to the originating house for concurrence. It may be killed by either house, or if the two houses cannot agree on its form, it may go to a conference committee which works out a compromise.

After reading this, I looked up at Mary and gulped.

"Right," she said, answering the question in my eyes.

"It can be killed in any of these steps. It's not a simple matter to pass a bill," she continued. "But when you're dealing with a law that will affect almost six million people, every legislator must have an opportunity to scrutinize it from every angle."

"What happens then when the House and Senate approve it?"

"It goes to the Governor for his signature. He has ten days to decide whether to sign it or veto it."

"Veto it?" I asked. "After the House and Senate approve it?"

"He has that right," she said. "But his veto can be overridden by a two-thirds majority vote in both the House and Senate."

"When the Governor signs it does it then become a law?"

"Yes, usually in ninety days. But remember, Rita," Mary warned, "watch out for those roadblocks and hurdles."

For a moment the old spectre of *unconstitutional* swam before me. But I put it out of my mind.

"I'm not worried, Mary," I smiled. "I know the power of positive believing."

Three weeks later, Representative George Young called me; I rushed right down to his office, glad that the State House was relatively close to Brockton.

There was the bill, looking so official with its special number: *No. 1010.* I picked it up, hands trembling, and read: "The school committee of any city or town may permit any child attending its public schools to participate in voluntary prayer with the approval of such child's parents. . . ." The prayers would be held before the official opening of the school day. I noticed, however, that my name wasn't on it. Representative Young explained that other people, who felt the same way I did, also filed bills. They were combined into one bill, and this one carried the name of another Representative and a citizen, Representative Frederick Kenney of Uxbridge and Rosaire Rajotte. At first, I was a bit disappointed, but then felt that it didn't make any difference whose names were on it. The important thing was that a bill for school prayer was filed. I was also beginning to learn that bills are often the sum total efforts of many people working together for the same goal.

Now the bill would go before the Education Committee. "You should be there, Mrs. Warren, along with any friends who'd like to speak for it," recommended Mr. Young.

"How will I know when to go?"

"They will send you a card, because you filed a bill on the same subject."

In about a week the card came. A good friend, Marilyn Layton, one of the mothers who had been with us from the start, said that she would join me. She, Teresa, Anita, and I got into our old car and chugged off for the State House. As we drove into downtown Boston, I didn't say much.

"What's the matter, Mom?" asked Teresa. "You're acting like you're really worried."

"No, Teresa, I am praying." I felt as if I, myself, were going on trial!

But when we stepped into the room where the Education Committee met, I relaxed. It was a friendly atmosphere. The committee members sat around a big table. The chairman was a woman Senator, Mary Fonsica, who introduced us, and the committee began to discuss the bill.

The chairman said, "As far as I'm concerned, this bill is the wish of many people, and I move that we record it favorably."

When we left, I felt sure the bill would go to the House of Representatives the next day. I called to check, remembering the Representative's words: "Ride herd on it, Mrs. Warren."

It turned out to still be in the Education Committee. Three days passed. Nothing. Then five days. Soon it would be a week.

"Is it going to die in the committee?" I wondered. As I fretted about it, Teresa said, "Mom, why don't you talk to them about it?"

"The committee members?"

"Sure. You said the government works for us. Well, doesn't that mean they represent us, too?"

"Of course." I thought, *Here I go again, thinking they were some kind of unapproachable people who would look down on me.*

I got a list of their names from Representative Young and began phoning them, reminding them of the bill.

A week later Mr. Young informed me that it went to the House of Representatives.

Representative Mary Fantasia told me what to watch for now. When a bill enters the House, it first goes to the Clerk of the House. He is the one who determines the priority of the bills, which ones go on to what day's docket for debate. His office is in the State House. From time to time, I would phone him to find out when our bill would go before the House. He didn't seem to resent it. I've always found that when you approach people on a friendly basis, most will respond in kind.

After about two or three days, in late June 1970, the bill was ready to go before the House.

I'll never forget that day. Marilyn Layton, Anita, Teresa, and I sat around our kitchen table, holding hands, and praying.

As we prayed, the 240 men and women representing the people of Massachusetts from the fish wharves of Boston to the Berkshires in the west were assembling for their 11:00 A.M. roll call. At this time, each representative gets a copy of the calendar for the day. This is a printed booklet listing all of the bills up for discussion that day.

The actual floor debate and voting doesn't start until 1:00 P.M. About 12:45 P.M., Marilyn, Anita, Teresa, and settled ourselves in seats in the visitors' gallery. We wanted to be sure we were there when the bill came up.

As we waited, I leafed through the calendar for the day, and noticed there were about forty bills for discussion. Forty bills! I did some quick figuring. That was about ten bills an hour. How much time would our bill get? Certainly, some would require less discussion than others. For example, one of the bills I saw listed was to make cranberry juice the "official beverage" of the Commonwealth. That should pass easily, I thought.

Finally the session started. It was fascinating to watch. When it came time for a particular bill, the Clerk, who sits next to the Speaker of the House, stood up and read the entire document in a loud voice.

Then the debate began. Sometimes, as with the cranberry juice, there was no debate. At other times, discussion waxed fast and furious with various representatives standing to argue their views. Then, after everyone had had his say, the vote was taken.

And then I saw the electric light bulbs in use, sometimes red predominating, other times green. *What would be the predominant color for our bill?* I worried.

Finally, our school-prayer bill was called. We all sat up. My heart was pounding. The debate started.

One representative said that he was against the bill. Approval, he said, would bring discredit to the House since the United States Supreme Court had ruled that such prayers were unconstitutional.

"But this is for *voluntary* prayer," another counter-argued. "No one is proscribing prayers."

I wanted to shout, "Let the children pray in their own words!" But, of course, I couldn't. We had to keep quiet. It was now out of our hands—or was it?

I whispered to the others and we all bowed our heads and prayed. We knew this was the strongest force in the State House.

The debate went on, men arguing pro and con. Some of their reasoning I couldn't understand. One man said that the arguments questioning the constitutionality of the bill were similar to the ones he raised questioning the constitutionality of the anti-Viet Nam war bill. The important thing to me was that he was for the prayer bill.

On it went, the four of us sitting at the rail watching the serious activity on the floor. I watched the Speaker as he controlled the debate. I noticed how he was always careful to recognize the first Representative to arise to speak. Sitting in front of the podium were the page boys who from time to time would go to the desk of a Representative upon his call.

Finally, they were ready to vote. I clutched my daughters' hands, and again bowed my head.

Suddenly Teresa nudged me. "Mom, look!" She pointed to the board; it was lighted up like a Christmas tree, and there were more green lights than red ones. Oh, that blessed green! When the official count was made, 207 Representatives had voted for voluntary prayers in public schools. Only 17 had voted against it. The rest had abstained.

We walked out of the building praising the Lord.

That evening as Teresa, Anita, and I sat around the kitchen table talking about the strong feelings some of the Representatives seemed to have against prayer, Teresa laughed. "That reminds me of a story I just heard. A school teacher walked into her classroom one morning and found all her students kneeling together in the corner. She rushed over, calling, 'Children, children, what are you doing?' One kid looked up over his shoulder and said, 'We're shooting dice, teacher.'" Teresa rolled her eyes and continued: "'Oh, thank goodness,' gasped the teacher. 'I thought you were praying!'"

We laughed. And then Teresa asked seriously: "Mom, what if we get the school prayer in Massachusetts. What about the rest of the country?"

She had a good point, and one I had long thought about.

"Well, Teresa," I said, "the way I look at it is this. It will make news everywhere that finally children get a chance to pray in school. Other people will take heart, and try to do the same thing in their own state.

"It's the spirit of the thing that counts," I continued. "A victory like this could counteract that terrible hopeless spirit cast over the country by the Supreme Court decision. You remember how some of those Representatives talked about it.

"But let's get ready for bed now," I ordered. "We've got a big day tomorrow. And besides," I added with a wink at Teresa, "you'll want to get your hair washed, won't you?"

And the next day was a big day. For that was when the bill would come up for debate in the Senate.

That afternoon found us sitting in the gallery of the Senate Chamber. Again we were early, and I had an opportunity to study this historic room, which is located directly under the gold dome of the Capitol building. Two Revolutionary muskets, one British and one American, hang on the wall. On the other is a portrait of President Calvin Coolidge who was a former President of the Senate, and flags from the Revolution occupy niches in the wall. The forty desks of the Senators compose a large semicircle almost filling the room.

Teresa nudged me as the session was opened with a prayer by the Chaplain of the Senate.

When the prayer bill came up, again there was a long debate. In fact, there seemed to be so much argument against it that I was frightened. How could they argue about children opening their school day with prayer when they have, in effect, just done the same thing themselves?

I did something I shouldn't. Up on the wall are large words that say: GOD SAVE OUR COMMONWEALTH. I stood up, leaned over the rail and pointed vigorously at the sign. Some of the Senators, who I knew were favorable to the bill, noticed me, smiled, nodded, and went back to the fray. Others, wondering what their associates were looking at, stared up at me. As they did, I pointed to the prayer written on the wall above them.

I could have been ejected from the visitors' gallery for doing this, and later wondered at myself. But I just couldn't help it.

Finally, it came time to vote. Since there were fewer Senators, a vote-indicator board wasn't used here. Instead, all those in favor would stand and say *aye*. But when the vote was called, I was surprised. Instead of *ayes* and *nayes,* it was an acclamation in favor of the bill! I stood up myself and said, "Hallelujah!"

Later, as we talked with my friend, Representative Mary Fantasia, she explained that it still had a way to go to be a law.

"Now, the Clerk of the Senate will send it back to the House for what they call a *reading,"* she said.

"Not for another debate?" I said.

"No," she smiled. "But it is a formality to clear the bill with the House to make sure that each group has agreed to the same thing. Sometimes the wording gets changed through amendments," she added, "and it is especially important that both houses agree to whatever changes have been made."

A few days passed and by keeping in contact with Representative George Young, through whom I originally filed the bill, I learned that it went to the Governor to be signed.

"Will he sign it right away?" I asked.

"Probably not," he said. "Remember, he has ten days in which to do it, so don't hold your breath. And don't forget, Rita," he added, "that after he signs it, it takes ninety days for it to become effective as a law."

I couldn't stand the waiting for it to be signed. Days went by, and no word on the bill from Governor

Francis Sargent. Why was he stalling? I wondered.
Finally, I could stand it no longer. Remembering
George Young's words, "Mrs. Warren, you will have to
push hard for this bill," I made a big sign saying: THE
GOVERNOR WON'T SIGN THE PRAYER BILL, and stood in
front of the State House. In a way, I realized it was silly,
but I had to do something, and it did give me an opportunity to tell the people who came by what was going on.

Finally, late in the afternoon on the tenth day, a man
hurried down the steps of the State House toward me.

Oh-oh, I wondered, *is this a guard to chase me off?*

It turned out to be a man who identified himself as
the Governor's secretary. "Mrs. Warren," he said, "you
can go home now. He has signed it."

Now I had to wait ninety days for the law to become
effective. Those three months were difficult times in my
life. I was like a child anxiously waiting for Christmas
to come. I tried to forget about it by throwing myself
into my housework. I even repainted the kitchen.

Thirty days passed, forty-five, fifty, sixty . . . in
agonizing slowness. Then Teresa, usually the cool one,
also started getting anxious. "After all, Mom," she
laughed, "I'm the one who's going to benefit."

But I still found myself crossing off the days on the
calendar. I remember it was getting close to that red-
letter day I had marked on my calendar as the ninetieth
day, when it happened. It was quiet in the house that
afternoon. I heard the newspaper boy come by and
went out and picked up the paper. How nice, I thought,
it will be to read the newspaper casually again. Always
before I had to hurriedly scan it for news on legislation.
Now I could relax and even enjoy the department-store
ads.

I settled back in the lounge chair and began reading.
After finishing the front page, I turned to the inside.
Hmmm, I thought, *Filene's is having a sale.* And then
something about a news item to the side caught my at-

tention. I really wanted to read the ad, but something in the headline nagged at me, and my eyes turned to it.

I dropped the paper and sat there in shock.

Was it true? I picked up the paper and read it again. The news was like a blow to my face. Our school-prayer law would *not* be implemented in the state. The Attorney General had declared that school prayer was unconstitutional and thus the law would not be implemented.

I immediately phoned my friend, Representative Mary Fantasia.

"Yes, Rita," she said sadly, "I'm afraid that it's all too true. He is within the law. You know what they keep saying: It's not constitutional."

I hung up the phone, anger and resentment flooding me. *Why?* I cried to myself. *Why have I been wasting my time like this? Have I been misreading the Lord's will for me? Or will school prayer always be a will-o-the-wisp which people will continually strive for, but never quite reach?*

8.

Picking Up the Pieces

Weeks had gone by, and now all I wanted was to forget the bill. Some people had told me that one person "couldn't fight City Hall," and I was beginning to think they might be right. At this point I didn't even want to be reminded of my efforts. And our kitchen and family room were reminding me of it constantly, being strewn with all the papers and letters resulting from our ill-fated school-prayer news coverage.

So one gray afternoon in February, I decided to clean everything up and put it away for good. As I stuffed papers into boxes, my eye happened to catch the child's handwriting on one sheet. I recognized it as a letter that had come some time ago and I remembered how much it had moved me then. I picked it up and reread it:

Dear Mrs. Warren,

I would like to commend you for your courage to get on television and express your opinion. I am sure you said exactly what many wish they had the courage to say. People may think that I am still too young to express my opinion, but I know that I believe in God and I hope when my children are school age that there will be prayers in the schools.

Since only a handful of atheists can remove

prayers from the schools, maybe with our backing, you can put them back in again. Thank you.

> Yours truly,
> DEBBIE LA BELLE, GRADE 8
> 13 years old

I sat there holding the letter for a long time. "Thank
you, Honey," I whispered. "Perhaps—perhaps with en-
couragement like this, I just might try again—someday."

Suddenly the ringing phone awoke me from my
reverie.

"Hi, Rita," spoke an animated voice that I seemed
to remember. "This is Tom Larson from Channel 38.
How would you like to debate Madalyn Murray O'Hair
again?" A half-hour ago I probably would have given
him a cold *no!* But now my spirits had risen. I am sure
that God had put that letter from little Debbie in my
hand. "Of course, Tom," I laughed. "Anytime!"

After I hung up the phone, I turned back to the
papers. Instead of stuffing them away, I thought I'd
better reorganize them. As I moved a stack of correspondence, again, as if He had placed it there, I saw
a memo. It was one which Madalyn had written me a
year ago in answer to a letter I had sent, reminding her
that I was praying for the return of her son Bill. No
one yet knew where he was after he had left home.
Along with my letter I had enclosed a prayer card:

> "God grant me the serenity to accept the things
> I cannot change, courage to change the things I
> can and wisdom to know the difference."

She had returned the card with a note:

> "Your prayer card intrigues me. You do not
> abide it, yet you send it to me. The first twelve

words here are in direct and violent contradiction with the Rita Warren I know. I like you!"

You're not reading me right, Madalyn, I smiled to myself. *My part of that prayer is for courage to change the things I can.* Now, even more, in my heart, I knew that somehow, someway, we would put the school-prayer bill into effect.

Later that week, Madalyn and I once again met under the hot lights of the TV studio. Again, our debate was even. She kept her firm stand, and I kept mine. One of the questions directed to Madalyn was: "Why do you seem to like Rita Warren so much?" Her answer was: "Because Rita possesses a rare gift, and that is sincerity."

Again, I felt we understood one another.

During the program we found a moment to talk. I thought I noticed an unusual sparkle in Madalyn's eyes. I asked her about her son Bill. "Ah," she said, "you remember my son Bill?"

"Of course."

"Well, he's home."

My heart leapt with joy. Bill had returned to his family. He had been up in Canada and, after much soul-searching, decided to come home. "I'm so happy," she breathed.

I jumped up and hugged her. "Oh, Madalyn!" I rejoiced. "I'm happy too. You have your son back. My prayers were answered!" And then (I'm sure it was the Holy Spirit who led me) I invited her to my home for dinner. A little to my surprise since—after all, I was the enemy camp—she accepted. "Why, Rita," she smiled. "How nice of you!"

As we headed toward my house I wondered how Madalyn would react to it. In my front yard is a flood-lighted statue of Jesus with His arms extended in blessing. Over the door is a sign: GOD IS FOR REAL, MAN!

However, as we stepped out of the car, Madalyn didn't seem to notice, and I supposed she dismissed it as "some of Rita's folklore." I was later to learn, however, she had noticed and respected my life-style by making no comment.

During the evening I learned more about Bill, his family, Madalyn's younger son, Garth, who was now sixteen, and her granddaughter, Robin. Madalyn also told me about her husband, Richard, who is a totally disabled World War II Marine veteran who had lost the top of his skull at Guadalcanal. "It's now protected by a silver plate," said Madalyn, "and I worry about him. He can't tolerate the sun. The silver plate actually becomes hot and his scalp blisters."

She told how they raise flowers, vegetables, and fruit trees in the backyard of their home in Austin, Texas. And then our talk turned to happenings in the world today. I discovered that Madalyn detests communism and expresses concern about people being duped into letting those who believed this ideology take over their countries.

"Why, Madalyn," I exclaimed, "I'm surprised."

"Why?" she asked.

"I guess I thought all Atheists were Communists."

She threw her head back and laughed heartily. "Well," she smiled, recovering her composure. "You are looking at an Atheist who *isn't*."

Anita and Teresa had long gone to bed, and still we talked. She had given me her own book about the early days of her struggle to get prayer out of school. I asked her some questions about it. She replied, "I just didn't believe he had to stand there with the rest of the children and say prayers when he is an Atheist," she said. "And then to top it off," she laughed, "when I told the school authorities that, they said that it would be compulsory for him to stand with the rest, maintain an attitude of reverence, and just move his lips as if he were saying prayers!"

I was laughing too, but not at the same thing. To my-self I thought, "Here Madalyn kept her son Bill out of school because he *had* to say a prayer, and I was keep-ing Teresa out because she *couldn't* say her prayers."

In some other ways our stories were parallel. I had been arrested; Madalyn was harrassed and arrested on related charges. We both had been in trouble for our beliefs. But I had never suffered as Madalyn and her family did.

I asked her if her book was really true. She replied, "I can't begin to count the times young Bill came home beaten bloody. One time he went to the shopping center to get something for his ham-radio set. When he came out of the hardware store a group of boys was waiting for him. 'Hey, here's the commie from our school!' one shouted. Bill headed toward the bus stop paying no at-tention to them. The gang built up as they followed, baiting him: 'Jesus loves you, Commie. Where's your mama today, Atheist? Hey, yellow, why don't you stop?'

"Finally as they danced in front of him, Bill re-treated into the Five and Ten, pleading with the clerks to call the police. None did. He bolted out of the store, but the gang caught him. They pinned his hands behind him, and beat his stomach. He broke free, and they followed, striking him with heavy belt buckles. Finally, he escaped into a bus that had stopped. When he got home, his back was bleeding through his shirt."

Madalyn sat for a moment silently, then added, "And all done in the name of religion."

"I'm sorry, Madalyn," was all I could say. The house was quiet. Our dog sprawled on the rug, snoring in his sleep. I asked Madalyn to go on.

"I won't go into all the times they vandalized our house and cars," she continued. "Smashed windows, trampled flowers. But why . . . *why?*" she asked. "Why did they have to do that to little Garth's kitten?" She elaborated that when Garth was eight years old his kitten disappeared one night. The next night it was thrown on their porch, strangled in vindictiveness by someone in the neighborhood.

"Garth crawled into my lap, crying, 'Everybody hates me, Mother. I didn't do anything, Mother. I didn't do anything!' "

I couldn't keep back the tears, as I listened to Madalyn.

She regained her composure. "Oh, one night a shot was fired into our house," she said. "But what really got us was the mail. The filthy, obscene letters were bad enough. But the ones that scared us were the death threats. There was one particular person whose writing I came to recognize. He started out with general threats, and each week or so his following letters built up explanations as to how he would kill me. Finally, one letter really frightened me for the entire last page was: *I will kill you. I will kill you, kill you, kill, kill, kill.*"

My heart cried as I heard these things, knowing that they were done by people thinking they were doing it in the Name of Jesus Christ.

"O Jesus," I prayed within myself, "forgive them."

As Madalyn talked, I guessed that her cause would have never reached the Supreme Court, if she had been given true Christian love from the beginning. It would have remained a minor affair in one school. But I could see how hate accomplished evil. It invaded those people who opened themselves to destructive forces through their anger.

I also winced as I heard of so-called evangelists practically forcing their way into Madalyn's house to shove tracts at her, and shout Scripture at her. *Oh,* I thought to myself, *if they had just offered her love and a kind word, Jesus could have walked right in with them.* As we talked, I spoke of Jesus frequently, but only in terms of the wonderful things He had done for me.

Before we realized it, it was 2:00 A.M.! As we stood up Madalyn was silent for a moment.

"Jesus is very real to you," she said, turning to me. "You discuss Him as if He were in this room."

"He is, Madalyn; He is."

The next morning I took her to Logan Airport. Somehow we both knew that we had cemented a strong friendship. As I watched her plane take off, swing wide over Boston harbor and then head for Texas, I prayed, "God bless you, Madalyn. May you get home safely."

When I returned from the airport and drove into my driveway, one of my neighbors happened to be walking by. I waved and called, "Good morning!" To my surprise, she kept her chin up and looked straight ahead and walked on. Later, I commented on this to Teresa. She said, "Yes, it's because she heard that Madalyn Murray O'Hair stayed here overnight."

I sat down in the same chair that I had been sitting in last night, when Madalyn and I had talked. "O Lord," I prayed, "if we could only rid ourselves of hate." I almost smiled to myself, thinking how a year ago I thought I hated the woman who was my guest last night. I didn't even know her, and yet I disliked her. And yet—now that I knew her—I could see that she was a child of God just as I am.

"O thank You, Lord," I said, "for delivering me from the spirit of hate."

And I'm sure that it is a spirit—a bad one. I saw what it could have done to a young man, who only a few years ago had fought a life-and-death struggle with hate in the very bedroom in which Madalyn slept last night. Perhaps this story will help convince those who hate Atheists (or anyone else who does not think as they do) that they are entertaining a most destructive spirit. There is only one spirit more powerful—the love of God we can give through Jesus Christ.

The young man was my sister's son, Tony, who was eighteen years old when it happened. He and a boy had a fight, and when it was over and Tony was walking away, the enraged boy picked up a baseball bat and swung it hard down on Tony's head. Tony crumpled to the ground, his head split open. An ambulance rushed him to the hospital, and in the emergency room the doctors thought he was dead. However, they detected a flicker of life, and they rushed him into surgery where they worked for hours, carefully picking shattered skull fragments from deep within his brain.

Finally, after days of intensive care, it looked as if Tony was going to live. But the entire right side of his body was completely paralyzed and he had lost his speech.

After many weeks in the hospital, Tony was ready to come home. But it was not the same bright-eyed young man I knew. He was a vegetable, with listless eyes staring at the ceiling. My heart went out to him and knowing that my sister had a large family, I offered to take him into my house. We had a spare bedroom, and she lived close enough so she could see him regularly.

After he came to live with us, I would sit with him day after day, and I could see a terrible thing take place. As he lay there, his head swathed in white bandages, his eyes lost their empty look, and began to smoulder with hate. Dark fires burned in their depths and his jaw began to tighten. As he recovered physically, the memory of how he came to be in such a condition freshened.

With his left hand Tony could laboriously write a few words on a pad. This is how we communicated. I gasped in fright when I first picked up the pad. On it was scrawled the name of the boy who had hit him and the words: KILL. KILL. KILL.

"Tony," I would softly plead, "don't hate. Have faith in God and He will help you."

But he would only turn his head to the wall, and clench his left hand. And always on the pad I would find those terrible words.

I didn't know what to do. Finally, one night I was led to put a Bible on the table next to him. "You'll find your answer in it," I told him. But he wouldn't look at it. It lay at his bedside untouched for two weeks. In the meantime, I kept praying that Jesus would take this hate from Tony's heart.

One morning I walked in with his breakfast to find him lying on his side, reading the Bible. He looked up at me sheepishly. I said nothing. That evening he showed me the part he had been reading. It was from Colossians, . . . *as the Lord has forgiven you, so you also must forgive* (3:13 RSV). The words seemed to have reached him.

"Tony," I explained, "it is far greater to forgive than to kill." His eyes lost some of their fire and he began to read his Bible every night. And soon his notes were coming to me thick and fast. WAS THIS REALLY TRUE? HOW CAN I FORGIVE WITH HATE IN MY HEART? WILL GOD'S SON REALLY HELP ME TO FORGIVE?

Carefully, I explained the answers to Tony. And then we began to pray together. A strange thing happened. As the hate left Tony's eyes, something began to happen to his body. One morning, he proudly showed me that he could wiggle the fingers on his right hand. Slowly, but surely, feeling began to return to his body. And then one evening I accidentally bumped him and he let out a little *ouch!*

We looked at each other in astonishment, and I began to clap my hands and cry. His voice was returning. One of his first sentences was, "Thank You, God." In two months Tony was almost normal.

His doctor couldn't understand it. "All I can say," he said, "it's really a miracle."

When Tony was up and about, it came time for him to appear in court against the boy who had struck him. I took him aside the night before. "Tony, you owe God your life. Now you must do something for Him."

"What?"

"Forgive that boy in court."

He looked down at the floor. I could see terrible conflict in his face. I knew that forgiving someone in your heart was one thing, but to confess this before other people, especially when vengeance was so easily and legally at hand, was quite another.

Tony gave me that quick smile and said, "I'll see, Aunt Rita. I'll see what God wants me to say, and I will say it."

As he walked out of my door toward his home, I prayed that he would not let God down.

In court the next day it was a tense scene. There stood Tony, his terrible scar still partially showing under his hair, and there stood the boy who did it, looking sullen, defiant, his eyes to the floor.

The judge asked Tony if he would press charges. Tony turned toward the boy, gave him a long look, and said: "No, your honor. I forgive him. I forgive him."

Tony's attacker became pale. He leaned forward onto the table where he sat. "Don't do this to me, Tony," he cried. "Don't do this to me!"

At that moment I was shown clearly the truth of His message: "Forgiving your enemy will heap living coals on his head." (*See* Romans 12:20.)

The boy was given a very light sentence. "I'm sentencing you so lightly," said the judge, "because Tony has forgiven you."

That happened in 1968. And as I thought back on that time, I looked toward the bedroom where Tony found God. Today he is a bright, intelligent young man, physically perfect in every respect.

I thought of all the people in this world who hate— and, yes, those who hate Atheists. How I wished I could bring them to meet Tony. And then, as I thought of this, I realized that this is not necessary. They all have Someone standing right at their side right now, patiently waiting.

As I sat there, I also realized that I could not resent

the school superintendent, the legislators, the lawyers, and all those who would not allow prayer back in the school. I could only do one thing: Love them, and in loving them, I knew that some way—somehow—this mountain would be moved. I knew then that I would try again, even if it meant repeating the whole ordeal of filing another bill in the State Legislature.

9.

One Last Hope

But the tension mounted.

And now, as I stood at the foot of my mountain, it not only looked quite immovable but threatening.

Criticism heightened, as news of my prayer campaign increased. I couldn't bring myself to file another bill yet, but I had been doing a lot of speaking on school prayer. Some of the letters that came in our mail I immediately destroyed. I did not want Teresa to see the hate and venom with which they were written. I wondered if in some strange way these might be the same people who had written to Madalyn Murray O'Hair!

But Teresa did not escape the harrassment. One afternoon she rushed into the house, ran into her room, and threw herself on the bed crying. I sat down next to her and soothed her. "Mama," she sobbed, looking up at me through tears, "I'm tired of people making fun of you and calling you a 'crazy fanatic.' "

Again, there was the strange parallel to Madalyn. I remembered from her book how they had bothered her son, when she took a public stand for her belief.

"Teresa," I soothed, stroking her long, black hair. She was becoming a tall, attractive girl. "I don't care what they say about me," I said. "All I care is what God thinks of me. As long as I try to do what He wants, I don't care what any one calls me."

Then a cold chill clutched my heart. I held Teresa

back from me, and looked into her eyes. "Has anyone tried to hurt you?"

She shook her head, then shrugged. "All I get is kids laughing at me and hollering, 'Here comes the prayer girl!' " She wiped her eyes and tried to smile.

It was time, I decided, that Teresa go back to school. It was now September 1971. She had been out of school a year. True, she had been keeping up with her classes through her special tutoring. But in good conscience I still could not let her return to a school in which prayer is forbidden.

"How about Cardinal Spellman High School?" she asked.

"But the tuition?" I worried.

"Don't worry, Mom. I can earn it."

And Teresa did. She got a job in a nearby doughnut shop working afternoons. She would rush home from school a little after 2:30 P.M., take a quick bite of lunch, and then dash over to the doughnut shop, where she worked from 3:00 until 7:00 P.M. She also worked all day Saturday. That, her homework (and washing her hair), kept her busy.

In the meantime, we continued to get by on what I made working in a bridal shop, and the child-support payments from Leverett. Though the payments were limited, I knew that he was doing what he could. When I couldn't find work, there was welfare.

I was presently working evenings in the bridal shop. This left my days free to work on the prayer campaign, handling correspondence, telephone calls, and planning meetings. I thank God for the people He sent to help. Our team had solidified into an efficient group of some twenty workers, including youths, mothers, a few fathers, and some older folks. The more criticism we got, the harder they worked. I noticed with a pang, however, that Teresa was now biting her nails. She had never done this before.

Some of the criticism came to me in letters from thoughtful and well-informed people. For example, some wrote me arguing that the Supreme Court did not stop children from praying quietly on their own at their desks, if they wished. My answer was that little children might well feel they could not do even this under the "You can't pray here!" cloud which now hung over public schools. That was how far the pendulum had swung.

But it did bother me that extremists were not the only ones who opposed prayer in schools. In order to do my job right, I at least needed to understand the thoughts of those opposing school prayer. As best as I could, I studied all the arguments against school prayer and condensed them into the following points:

1. The state must not be allowed to influence school children in their religious beliefs. Suppose, for instance, that the state began to influence children to become Jews, or Catholics, or Protestants—any one religion. Citizens of all faiths must be on guard against this happening.
2. Training a child in specific religious beliefs is not the function of a public school.
3. Religion should be taught in the home, Sunday school, parochial school, and place of worship.
4. "Neutrality" between church and state. Much of the Supreme Court's majority ruling was based on this. The judges were careful to stress that the primary effect of public education was to neither advance nor inhibit religion.

Well, I could certainly agree with some of these points. I didn't want the state dictating religion to my children. It followed that "teaching religion" was the job of the individual not the state.

But the real problem came with the last point, about

"neutrality." I went back to the opinion of Supreme
Court Justice Potter Stewart, one of the judges dis-
senting to the majority ruling and reread it.

Justice Stewart maintained that "a compulsory state
educational system so structures a child's life that if
religious exercises are held to be an impermissible activity in schools, religion is placed at an artificial and
state-created disadvantage. Viewed in this light, permission of such exercises for those who want them is
necessary if the schools are truly to be neutral in the
matter of religion. And a refusal to permit religious
exercises thus is seen, not as the realization of state
neutrality, but rather as the establishment of a religion
of secularism, or at least, as government support of the
beliefs of those who think that religious exercises
should be conducted only in private."

I put the book down and thought. There was no
doubt about it. A Supreme Court judge was saying that
his own court's ruling was *not* neutral; rather, it was
biased in favor of those who did not want any prayer
in school.

I thought about all the many things I have seen happening in the past seven years that worried me: the
slackening in morals, the growing filth in magazines
and movies, the winking at dishonesty. Even vandalism
by children seemed to be increasing in all parts of the
country. What about truthfulness, politeness, the
Golden Rule, and good sportsmanship? I wondered.
Didn't all these graces that we expect the school to
help build within our children stem from God's teach-
ings?

In view of all this, was it right for the highest court in
the land to go along with the lowest nonreligious common denominator, and try to force all American children into the grayest possible moral frame? This
certainly isn't what our founding fathers meant by a
guaranteed freedom to worship—where, when, and
how a person chooses!

I began to feel firmer than ever on my ground. No, not in any way, would I want public schools to dictate or even advise children on matters of religion. But by the same token, I deeply felt that children should have voluntary expression of their faith. And if they wanted to pray in school, then let there be a time set aside in which they might do so.

By now I felt I was better able to formulate my own feelings on the matter. And soon I was at the kitchen table writing a letter to the editor of our local paper. In a sense this letter was to become my platform on school prayer:

> To separate all religious expression during a large part of the children's daily activities is to deny them their rights to the free exercise of religion and the freedom of speech, while at the same time, creating the establishment of a single religious belief: namely, Atheism.

It was printed. And as I sat in our living room reading it, I had to chuckle at that last sentence. For Madalyn Murray O'Hair had actually founded a religion for Atheists. She declared herself a "bishop" and her husband, Richard, a "prophet," and sought converts to their Poor Richard's Universal Life Church. In her newspaper announcements, she told Atheists that "you can help your new Universal Life Church, your new religion, and at the same time you can profit in your relationship with the Internal Revenue Service."

I smiled as I could see that Madalyn was using "religion" in a sense that it was a set of beliefs, like humanism. So, in denying that there is a God, her Universal Life Church actually enters a religious realm.

Oh-oh, Madalyn, I laughed to myself, *if word gets out that the Supreme Court case was based on one person's view of religion, they might be in trouble.*

Meanwhile, I continued to be encouraged in my

campaign by what other people were doing. By this time I had assembled quite a scrapbook of news clippings and booklets:

- Billy Graham said in a news article that he was against state-imposed forms of prayer or demanding that all pray. "But," he said, "students should have the right to pray silently on a voluntary basis, or to repeat prayers used in the Supreme Court, or before Congress."
- Norman Vincent Peale, through his Foundation for Christian Living put out a little booklet called *One Nation Under God,* which underlined America's historic dependence on God's guidance. I particularly remember one part in which he told about the terrible deadlock among our nation's founders as they were trying to write the Constitution in Philadelphia in 1787. The future looked black and then Benjamin Franklin rose from his chair and declared: "Gentlemen, I have lived a long time and am convinced that God governs the affairs of men. If a sparrow cannot fall to the ground without His notice, is it probable that an empire can rise without His aid? I, therefore, move that prayers imploring the assistance of Heaven be held every morning before we proceed to business."

They did just that; not long after a compromise was reached, and the United States Constitution was born —on the wings of prayer.

- The Union of Orthodox Jewish Congregations of America recommended that Nelson Rockefeller, then Governor of New York, sign the bill currently before him that was passed by his state's legislature, permitting brief, silent prayer, or reflection at the beginning of each school day.
  "In this period of silent devotion," their statement

read, "let every pupil think of the Almighty in terms of his faith and his parental religious heritage, and thusly invoke His protection for himself, his family, his country, and all mankind."

- In the meantime, while the weighty matters of law are being balanced, many people worry that classic Bible ethics are being placed at a *dis*advantage. What to do about it? School libraries, which carry books on many different religions including the occult and the state-religion of Communism, are free to carry Christian books too. An Ohio housewife, Evelyn Moffat, felt that it was wrong to allow other religions a strong voice in school libraries without giving Christianity its hour. In 1964, she launched a faith ministry which has distributed some twenty thousand Christian books appealing to all age groups to public-school libraries in nineteen states and Puerto Rico. (Christian School Books, P.O. Box 155, Hubbard, Ohio, 44425.) Schools report a high popularity of the books with students and no opposition.

- In a similar vein, teaching the Bible as literature in the English departments of public schools is becoming more prevalent every year. Dr. Joseph Forcinelli, of the University of Iowa's Summer Institute on Teaching about Religion, reports that school districts in at least twenty-five states offer courses in comparative religion or the history of religion. Many English teachers who find their "Bible As Literature" courses to be popular electives with students, initiated the course because they felt a knowledge of the Bible vital to the well-rounded, educated person. As the Supreme Court majority decision observed: ". . . one's education is not complete without a study of comparative religions or the history of religion and its relationship to the advancement of civilization."

- A woman called "the Bible lady," Mrs. James E. Howard of Owensboro, Kentucky, placed framed

copies of the Ten Commandments in fifteen school
libraries, and in 1971 also placed (with school-board
approval) on the desk of every teacher in the
system a copy of the King James Version of the
Bible. Her work inspired Mrs. C. W. Whittaker, a
member of the county PTA, to hang framed copies
of the Ten Commandments in seventeen county
school libraries.

Their activities are perfectly legal according to the
often-misunderstood intent of the Supreme Court
ruling.

I sat there with the scrapbook in my lap, thinking of
all the foggy contradictions that have blanketed the
school-prayer situation since 1963. All, I felt, illus-
trated the curse of the Supreme Court ruling that has
since haunted America, tainting anything connecting
religion and public school with the mark of illegality.
I am sure that the court justices did not intend for
this to happen. But happen it has, and every enemy
of God—such as the purveyors of pornography and the
advocates of violence—has taken advantage of the mis-
understandings to advance his own philosophy. The
more involved I became with this often dark subject,
the more grateful I was for Christian fellowship.

One of my biggest sources of inspiration was my
friend, John McCormack. By this time he had retired
as Speaker of the House of Representatives in Washington, and had set up offices in his home city of
Boston. Here he was able to keep in touch with friends,
and stay abreast of the political scene. In fact, anyone
could find him in his office from 1 P.M. to 5 P.M.,
where he was happy to greet them.

I'll never forget waiting in his reception room one
afternoon. Out of his office door he came walking with
a wizened little old man, who was poorly dressed. The
Speaker had an arm around the old man's shoulders
and seemed to be comforting him. I thought to myself,
Here is a man who associates with world leaders, and

yet still takes the time to cheer the heart of a tired old man.

Naturally, I'd stop in to see John McCormack whenever possible. And he always found time to ask me how the school-prayer battle was going. Yet, despite all the assurances from him and other friends, I still shuddered when I considered again trying to file a prayer bill in our state's legislature. Would it be worth all the trouble, all the weeks of work, and days in the galleries not only for myself but others? And then, after we struggled to push the stone to the top of the hill, would it again roll all the way back down on us? For there was no reason to think that someone wouldn't find the bill unconstitutional again.

One evening as I brooded on this, into the living room walked Anita, the child the doctors said would die as a baby or, at best, be a vegetable who would neither think, walk, nor talk. She switched on the television to "I Love Lucy."

As I watched her turn the dial to get the proper channel, I remembered her last operation. Teresa and I spent two hours on our knees in the hospital chapel. Teresa comforted me: "Don't cry, Mommy," she said. "Anita is in the arms of God." She pointed to a stained-glass picture at the front of the chapel. It was Jesus holding a little lamb in His arms.

Now as I sat in the living room, I leaned my head back and put myself into His arms. "O Father," I prayed, "do You want me to continue this work for prayer? Or by my defeat have You shown me I should stop? Either way, I relinquish myself to You. But Father, if it be Your will that I continue, please give me Your direction and strength."

I sat relaxed in the chair, my eyes closed, my arms spread out, palms up in supplication. Either way I *knew* He would fill me with His answer.

As I rested there, a word kept coming to me: *referendum.*

Referendum? What was that? I asked myself. I

couldn't remember hearing the word before. But somehow it seemed significant. It seemed to have something to do with voting. Well, I thought, the best way to find out was to go to someone who knows.

The next morning I went to the office of my State Representative. For some reason I felt I should go to him, even though I knew he wasn't fully sympathetic with school prayer. A handsome young man with Irish blue eyes and blond hair, he flashed me the smile that had helped him win his office.

"Mrs. Warren!" he exclaimed. "To what do I owe this honor?" He gallantly waved me into his office in such a way that I was the one who felt honored.

After we got settled, I asked him, "What is a referendum?"

"Oh," he said, leaning back in his chair, "that is simply putting a question before the people by placing it on an election ballot." He explained that that way legislators really know the people's opinion on a question, and from it are guided in their legislation.

Suddenly the sky opened and a bright illumination flooded me.

Of course! This was the difference. If it could be clearly shown that the majority of people in the state of Massachusetts wanted prayer in their public schools, wouldn't a public official be hard-pressed not to let it go into effect? I felt sure that even the Attorney General's opinion on the unconstitutionality of school prayer couldn't stand up against this kind of mandate!

Now I knew what I had to do. I looked at my Representative. "Then I'd like to file a bill to put the school-prayer question on the ballot for the next election."

He sat pensively for a moment, tapping a pencil against his chin. Then he looked up at me and smiled. "Well, Mrs. Warren, you know I don't quite agree with your thoughts on school prayer," he said. However, he pointed out that it was my right as a citizen to file a bill. And, as my Representative, it was his duty to file it for me.

He explained that I should get a large number of signatures from citizens requesting that prayer be put back into schools—at least 65,000 of them. Then I could present them to our state's Education Committee when asking that the question be placed before the people.

"Can I file for the November election?" I asked, my heart in my throat. I was looking at his wall calendar. The next election was November 7, 1972, just months away. I knew that I would have to make this election. The referendum now was our only hope. Otherwise we'd have to wait two more years. And that was too long to put things off. A lot can happen in two years. Our whole campaign could die.

My Representative didn't answer my question right away. He had turned to his desk, checked some papers, and then turned back to me shaking his head.

"I'm sorry, Mrs. Warren," he said, "but I'm afraid it's too late."

10.

Does the Public Really Want School Prayer?

The world seemed to shatter into little bits about me.

The Representative sat at his desk, his eyes fixed thoughtfully on the calendar. The big wall clock slowly ticked off dead minutes.

"There's nothing we can do?" I breathed.

"Well," he said, swinging his chair back to me. "It's past the deadline to file a bill for this legislative session." However, he said that perhaps we could take a chance with what's known as a "late-filed bill." It may or may not be heard, he said. He looked at me closely. "Do you want to try it?"

Did I want to try it! There was a pay telephone outside his office. And it must have been the busiest telephone in Boston that afternoon as I called our team. We needed 65,000 signatures in thirty days.

We spread out over the city, canvassing for signatures. We haunted the Commons, went to all the Protestant and Catholic churches we could reach. One Sunday, I attended all four masses at my own church to make sure we got everybody. Our cause became an ecumenical campaign with practically all Protestant ministers in Boston joining us.

It was tiring. And one day while hurrying up some steps, I tripped and sprained my ankle. My doctor recommended that I keep off of it. But I couldn't. We had plans to petition on Washington Street the next day. That morning I stood outside Filene's Department Store on crutches. An icy spring wind blew down the street and my ankle pain was excruciating. But in three hours our team got three thousand signatures. Everybody, it seemed, wanted a chance to put their vote *X* behind YES, WE WANT SCHOOL PRAYER on the ballot.

On awakening the next morning, I hesitatingly touched my bad foot to the floor and got a surprise. The swelling on my ankle had gone down completely! Moreover my foot had no pain at all. I called my doctor. Was it possible, I asked, for a sprained ankle to recover so quickly?

No, he said, medically it wasn't possible. "Thank you, doctor," I said, and smiled to myself thinking that medically, *no,* but spiritually, *yes.*

Finally, we had the signatures of 65,000 people, all asking that prayer be returned to the public schools. It was now June 1. Time was running short! On July 8 the legislature would close for summer recess. On top of that, the Democratic National Presidential Convention would begin the following Monday, July 11, in Miami. Many members of the House and Senate would be in a hurry, intent on getting to that important convention.

With the help of my Representative, I had already filed the late bill. It called for a referendum on the November 1972 ballot on the question of voluntary prayer recitation in the public schools. Then, with the strength of the signatures we had from 65,000 Massachusetts citizens speaking out for it, we had little trouble getting approval of the members of the Education Committee.

Days dragged by while I kept reminding the Clerk of the House of Representatives about the bill. Then my Representative phoned me. "Mrs. Warren, the prayer-referendum bill is scheduled to go before the House on Thursday, July 7."

July 7! That was cutting it close. If passed, it would go to the Senate on its last day before summer recess! But if it did not pass? I tried to dismiss the thought of its failing out of my mind. But from past experience, I knew that one tiny little thing in the legislative process could block a bill—like a grain of sand in a fine watch. If this bill were held up at all, there would be no referendum, no opportunity for citizens to vote on it this November, no mandate of the people on school prayer.

Moreover, I knew that it would be very easy for our bill to become smothered in the flood of other bills competing for the legislators' attention. I knew of many major bills waiting. They ranged from Governor Sargent's emergency Metropolitan Boston Transit Authority program and a bill increasing the legal minimum wage, to an omnibus prison-reform bill, not to mention a decision about selling state-lottery tickets on Sunday.

Wouldn't our referendum bill become a scrap of paper lost in the frenzied winds of the session's closing?

There was one thing I could do. I got on the phone and started calling every member of the House, urging them to vote for the bill. By the time I had reached the last names on my list it was after 11 P.M. I apologized but explained how important I thought it was.

July 7 arrived and my daughters, my friend Marilyn Layton, who had accompanied me on the other prayer bill two years ago, and I were up in the gallery of the House at 1:00 P.M. We watched anxiously but there wasn't too much of a debate and the bill passed by acclamation. All those glowing green lights looked so reassuring.

But as we sat there laughing together in relief, I reminded myself not to get too confident. The bill had two other hurdles: the Senate and the Governor's signature. But even surmounting these, would the question still get on the ballot? I remembered only too well having the rug pulled from under my feet two years ago, when the bill that seemed to be such a victory for school prayer ended up as a meaningless statement on the law book.

But now was no time to entertain negative thoughts. That evening I got on the phone and started calling all forty senators. "What are you doing, Mrs. Warren," asked one in mock desperation, "taking a roll call over the telephone?"

I'll never forget that final day, the last day before summer recess. If the bill didn't pass now, the prayer referendum would never make the November ballot. As we walked up the wide stone steps of the State House that sunny morning, I looked up past its big gold dome into the blue above and prayed hard. Directly under that gold dome was the Senate Chamber where it would all take place today.

The Senators' debate began hot and heavy. It was agonizing to see the men argue over the bill. Those arguing against it all seemed to use the Supreme Court ruling that it was unconstitutional. There was my nemesis again—*unconstitutional*.

I couldn't help but rise from my seat in the gallery, and stand at the rail—praying. Many of the senators who knew me very well by now kept looking up at me. When they did, I'd again vigorously point to the words on the wall of the chamber: GOD SAVE THIS COMMONWEALTH. One Senator called his opponent's attention to the words and stated, "Well, we have it right up there."

Finally, after an agonizing time, a vote was called. Thirty-two of the forty senators stood up to vote *yes!* for the referendum; I was standing with them up in the gallery, crying and praising the Lord.

Now we had to wait for the Governor to sign the bill. "Mama," said Teresa one day while we were waiting, "please promise me something."

"What is it, Honey?"

"Please don't stand out in front of the State House with a sign this time."

I laughed. "No, Honey, I promise."

On the fifth day Governor Sargent signed the bill.

Now it would be placed before the people on November 7, 1972. Question 9 on the ballot would ask the citizens to vote *yes* or *no* on whether the voluntary recitation of prayer should be authorized in the Massachusetts public schools.

And now our real work started.

We would have to campaign for this vote as effectively and as strongly as any party would for its candidate. Of course, I knew that winning this election would not insure prayer in the public schools. Another bill would have to go through the legislative process for that—and, this time, a bill worded to withstand any constitutionality scrutiny. But without this expression of the people behind us, filing any kind of bill for school prayer wouldn't be worth trying.

And we had less than four months in which to do it.

We started our campaigning by designing a poster urging people to vote YES ON QUESTION 9. We had two hundred of these printed up, using donated funds, and our youth workers took off with them in cars, on bicycles, and on foot, delivering one to every church in the Boston area. We were constantly on the phone with television and radio stations, begging them for editorials.

And many of the stations gave time to this important question. Sometimes they didn't quite fully agree with us, such as the general manager of WBZ-TV and WBZ Radio. They read this statement over the air as an editorial:

> That much-debated issue of school prayer has made its way on to the state election ballot this year. Question Nine will ask if you approve of the idea of voluntary recitation of prayer in the public schools.
>
> This vote is advisory only, and it can have no immediate impact on the law or public policy here in Massachusetts. The courts have ruled

that all forms of school prayer are unconstitutional. Backers of Question Nine are simply out to get grassroots backing for . . . voluntary school prayer. . . . As we've said before, we don't like to see the state ballot cluttered up with this sort of public policy question. But since it's there, we'll vote on it—and our votes will be on the *yes* side, with one major reservation.

We don't think any child should have any particular faith or religious view shoved down his or her throat in a public school. But the First Amendment to the Constitution, which separates church and state, also assures the free exercise of religion. Voluntary prayer sessions at the start of the school day seem to us to be in keeping with those guidelines. The emphasis has to be on the word *voluntary*—for school officials, teachers, and pupils. And to us that also means prayer in private and in silence. Prayer is a very personal matter. There's no reason to make a show of it. Question Nine uses the word "recitation" which could involve some public display or oratory. We object to that because it could put added pressure on children whose faith and views differ from the majority. Kids can be incredibly cruel to others who differ from the norm in situations like this.

This time around we'll join with those prodding Congress for a prayer amendment. But unless that amendment makes it emphatic that school prayer is to be both voluntary and private, we'll be on the other side when the votes really count.

This editorial gave me a lot to think about. I felt that recitation was important. I could see what this TV station editor meant: It would be wrong to force everyone to say the same prayer. I thought again about what Madalyn told me about her son being told to move his lips in unison with the other children.

We got other air-time appearances. Often we'd be

able to get right on a program and speak for five minutes on behalf of school prayer. On one of these occasions I was honored to appear along with Mr. John McCormack. He was very optimistic about the prayer vote, and when the interviewer asked him if he could predict the outcome, he said very matter-of-factly:

"I believe that 85 percent of the people will vote for it."

I turned to him in surprise. "Oh, Mr. McCormack," I said, "you're just trying to make me feel good!" Yet deep in my heart I knew that if the referendum was going to mean anything, it would have to win by a high percentage. Even a 60 percent in favor of prayer wouldn't carry a lot of weight with the legislators, I felt. And so I continued to pray.

Every step we took we depended on prayer. And this included getting the funds we needed to carry on the campaign. Practically all of them were coming to us in five-dollar and ten-dollar donations. Sometimes a twenty-five-dollar or even a fifty-dollar check would come in the mail, but that was an exception.

One Friday morning I awoke, knowing that we faced a real problem. We had an important mailing that had to go out that day and I had run out of stamps. We needed 600 stamps. I sat there on the edge of my bed and prayed, "Dear Lord, You know our need. Oh, thank You for filling it." By this time I had learned that once I had a firm direction from the Lord I should never use the word *if* in bringing my needs to Him. I felt that saying things such as, *"If* it be Thy will . . ."* indicated doubt, lack of assurance. And doubt, I felt, blocks us from responding fully to Him, so that we don't get His guidance and illumination in solving our problem. And so I have learned to approach Him in full faith knowing that I *will* be helped.

I believe God loves positive people who take Him at His word. As Jesus says, "Have faith in God. Truly,

I say to you, whoever says to this mountain, 'Be taken up and cast into the sea,' and does not doubt in his heart, but believes that what he says will come to pass, it will be done for him" (Mark 11:22 RSV).

So that morning I prayed the prayer of faith. And then, also knowing that faith without work(s) means nothing, I got into my car and began canvassing churches for the stamps. By 3 P.M. that afternoon we had 690 stamps and the letters were sent out in the late afternoon mail!

Some clergy were wonderful to us in our work. All faiths, all denominations helped us in every way they could. And at every opportunity, I spoke to congregations and pulpits were opened to us all over the Boston area from the south to the north shore.

As fall approached I had a strong sense of urgency that we must work harder than ever. As the lazy summer days waned, I'll admit that there were times when I felt like letting up a bit. After all, most people I talked to were in favor of school prayer. And I wondered if the speaking and the canvassing were all that necessary. But as this feeling began to come over me, I resisted it. I knew it could all be lost by letting up in the eleventh hour.

By October our prayer team all knew we were in the homestretch. And now we really went to town. We wrote and printed literature, including letters and mimeographed broadsides, which we passed out all over the city from the Boston Commons to the big shopping centers.

The newspaper reporters seemed to enjoy talking to us mothers as we distributed our literature. Perhaps it was because we didn't hold back anything when giving our statements. We had nothing to be afraid of.

One reporter laughingly said: "You're stepping on some big toes, Rita."

"What did he mean?" I wondered to myself. Perhaps he meant the large, organized groups such as some religious denominations that I had heard of which had come out against school prayer.

"There are no big toes," I laughed, smiling at him. "Only God has a big toe and *that's* the One I'm careful of."

One reporter, perhaps thinking of all the assassination attempts on people who got in the news during the past several years, warned me, "You could be shot, Mrs. Warren."

"I don't care," I said, "then I'll go home to Jesus." And to me that was true. By now Jesus had become such a Friend that I looked forward to being with Him all the time.

Late one night my phone rang. I picked it up to hear a familiar, jovial voice, "Well, I hear you're doing good in Massachusetts." It was Madalyn.

"So far it looks good," I laughed.

"Of course, you know I'll have to fight you," she chortled.

"Sure, Madalyn, you are welcome to the fight," I retorted, "but, of course, you know that you will lose!"

By mid-October five big billboards blossomed out along thruways and on top of buildings, one in Boston and the others in Brockton, Taunton, Hyde Park, and West Roxbury—all of them suburbs.

HELP RESTORE PRAYER
IN SCHOOL
VOTE FOR PRAYER AMENDMENT
QUESTION 9 ON THE BALLOT.

John Donnelly & Sons, an advertising firm, donated the billboards, and the printing was paid for by our young people, who got the money through donations or by working for it in part-time jobs.

Three days before the election I rented a loudspeaker, mounted it on top of my old car, and chugged through the streets of Boston and the suburbs every day, urging all those in earshot to vote "Yes on Question 9." When I rested my voice, I played "The Battle Hymn of the Republic" through a tape recorder.

Election fever was now high, and reporters stuck their heads into the car: "Who are you campaigning for, Mrs. Warren?" They knew what I was doing, but they always seemed to enjoy pulling my leg. Well, I could give it back to them.

"I'm campaigning for God—in case you don't know it," I said, "and my Candidate is a sure winner!"

I also traveled as much as I could through the state speaking in churches, schools, and colleges. I still made many mistakes in my English and never prepared a speech. But each time I would stand before an audience, I prayed that God would make the words come out right. He always did.

Finally, it was November 6, the day before the election. I had just finished making a speech, and it was late afternoon. Before heading home, I drove my car up to the brow of a hill. The sun was setting, and the western sky was ablaze with colors. I thought of the Berkshire Mountains out there, and the fact that I had not been able to make any of the communities in that far-western part of the state. And then the oppressive accusations began to berate me thick and fast. "You didn't make many towns in the north or the south either. And what about the Cape?" I felt terrible. Who was I to be so hopeful, when I had only covered a tiny part of Massachusetts? And then I remembered from whom these accusations came. I turned my back on the evil one and faced my everpresent Source of help. "O Jesus," I prayed, "I couldn't be everywhere. But *You* can. Please go into all those places and touch every heart."

I went to bed that night knowing that whatever happened, it was in His hands. I couldn't think of any better place for it to be.

Tuesday evening, voting day, I sat glued to my tele-

vision set. Early returns were coming in, and finally I
dozed off. But it was all there in the morning paper.

John McCormack was close in his prediction. Instead of his 85 percent forecast for the prayer-bill vote,
it was 84 percent. The people of Massachusetts had
voted to return prayer to the public schools by an over-
whelming majority—1,776,930 to 383,494.

I could hardly believe it. Yet deep down it seemed
like something I had expected all the time. The newspapers, television, and radio were alive with the news
all that Wednesday. Our phone rang constantly with
congratulations. And both girls were squealing with
delight.

But I knew the battle was only half over.

11.

Caring and Sharing With an Atheist

"Mama, will the children be able to say their prayers in school now?" It was Anita asking this question. She had helped so much in our electioneering, folding, sealing envelopes. Many times she answered the phone. She was so proud when she was able to do this. She spoke very slowly on the phone, but she always got the message.

"No, Anita," I said. "We will again have to file a bill for this just like we did two years ago."

Two years ago! I thought to myself. So much has happened since. Now Teresa was fifteen years old, Anita was twenty-two. I could hardly believe it. Where had my little girls gone? I looked into the mirror; my hair was getting gray. "Well," I thought, "what can one expect of a forty-four-year-old woman who has been carrying on a battle for the last three years." But I loved it. I had to admit I loved every minute of it.

Late one fall morning I went down to the State House to talk with Representative Mary Fantasia about the bill. She was so helpful to me.

After I sat down in her office, she said, "I have a surprise for you."

"A surprise?"

"The bill that you're after has already been filed."

"Filed?" I felt a quick surge of anger—as if someone had taken something away from me. And then I

quickly put it down. (By this time I was better able
to control my temper.)

"Yes," said Mary. "Representative Raymond M.
LaFontaine of Gardner has already put it through."

"Wonderful!" I said. "I don't care who filed it, as
long as it goes into the works. But one thing you know
for sure, Mary," I laughed. "You know that I will
fight for it with all my strength."

A few days later I saw the bill in printed form. There
it was on a 5 by 9 inch piece of paper:

Bill Number 4890
The Commonwealth of Massachusetts

An Act Allowing for a moment of meditation
for school prayer in the public schools

At the commencement of the first class of
each day in all grades in all public schools,
the teacher in charge of the room in which
such class is held shall announce that a
period of silence not to exceed one minute
in duration shall be observed for meditation
and prayer, and during any such period,
silence shall be maintained and no activities
engaged in.

A period of silence for meditation and prayer. I
said the words over softly. This was it. In God's own
way, working through Representative LaFontaine, He
had seen to the right wording for the bill. How could
anyone, even an Atheist, I thought, object to a period
of silence in which everyone could think or pray as he
wished?

I held the slip of paper to my heart and prayed: "Oh,
Lord, this is Your work. I know You will see it
through."

Then I noticed at the bottom of the bill this statement printed in small words: THIS DOCUMENT HAS BEEN PRINTED ON 100 PER CENT RECYCLED PAPER.

I smiled wryly to myself. I hoped this wouldn't mean that the bill would be like the paper on which it was printed, recycled again and again!

Early one morning, a few days after the bill was filed, I was sitting at my kitchen table over coffee. Teresa had already gone on to her classes at Cardinal Spellman High School, and Anita was playing with Lupo. I was thinking of all the work that lay ahead of me on the bill, being there at the debates, standing vigil in the galleries and—yes, I had to admit—the possibility that it might not make it.

But this time it would be different, I assured myself. *This time it would have the power of the people's desire behind it. Nothing,* I said to myself, *could stop it from becoming a law now.* As it turned out, I was somewhat naïve.

In the meantime, if I had any compunctions about completely getting behind the bill, they were all washed away by the "Christmas Guidelines" fiasco. To me, this was a prime example of what can happen when a civic body carries a concept of the 1963 Supreme Court decision to the extreme. And it made me all the more determined to see that our school-prayer bill got through.

I first read about the guidelines in our local paper. Our State Board of Education had issued them to each school system, urging a withdrawal from the classroom of religious displays, music, and pageants.

I asked a teacher friend about it. "Yes," she said, "that means things like manger scenes, Christmas plays, carols . . ."

"You mean the kids can't sing 'Silent Night'?"

"Nor 'The First Noel' or 'Hark, the Herald Angels Sing,'" she confirmed.

I could hardly believe it.

"My only hope," she continued, "is that these are

merely guidelines, not a definite ruling. Thus it's up to each school committee to interpret as it sees fit."

"But from what I have seen," I said, "it won't work out that way. These guidelines will become as solidly entrenched as law."

Fortunately, many others felt the same way. And Representatives Raymond Flynn, Mary Fantasia, and myself filed a bill to override the guidelines. Our bill would empower local school boards to decide how to celebrate Christmas and other festivals in their area. In the meantime, these guidelines were in effect through that Christmas of 1972. They were issued to the school superintendents, who take their orders from the state board. In many cases, we learned that the local school committees were never shown the guidelines. Instead, some superintendents handed down their own decisions.

And what no one ever dreamed would happen—did.

As the season started, many schools were pressured to remove every vestige of Christ's birthday. Other schools, confused by the whole situation, felt it safer to follow the "recommendations," in effect, accepting them as law.

One school system called their Christmas vacation a "winter vacation." In another school, children had to remove their paper angels and stars from classroom walls and throw them into the wastebasket. In several schools children were forbidden to sing "Silent Night" and other carols, or present a manger scene.

In our own home on Court Street, Christmas was celebrated as usual—an especially joyous time. A tall fragrant tree filled one corner of the living room, wreaths festooned the windows, and the Son of God was welcomed everywhere from lintel to mantle.

Into all these festivities stepped Madalyn Murray O'Hair. It came about when a Boston TV station invited both of us to participate in another television debate. Then a local college wanted us to debate before the students on the day after our television appearance.

I again invited Madalyn to spend the night at our house. We met at the studio, had our debate, and then set off for Brockton. As we drove home, I wondered how she would react to the tree? The star? The angels?

So I was a bit apprehensive when we drove up to the house—but the girls had outdone themselves. Out on the snow was a big sign.

WELCOME BACK, MRS. O'HAIR

When Madalyn stepped inside to be greeted with warm hugs from Teresa and Anita, she seemed as delighted as any child on Christmas morning.

"Oh, I love Christmas," she exclaimed, "I always have," she continued. "Why we have the biggest bang-up Christmas in our house that anyone can imagine."

As I stood there open-mouthed, she continued, "Only I call it Greetings of the Winter Solstice Season."

She explained that this is because Christmas falls close after the shortest day of the year—the winter solstice—the time originally regarded by the pagans as the rebirth of the sun, when the light began its conquering battle against darkness.

To her, she said it was still a time of rejoicing, that good-will and love will have a perpetual rebirth in the minds of men. She explained that her family has a tree as a symbol of the evergreen promise of nature, that they exchange gifts as a symbol of the "great gift of renewed life."

"And we sing and eat and dance and laugh," she added, "keeping the spirit of it for weeks before and weeks afterwards."

I decided that since it was Christmas, I wouldn't argue with Madalyn. We enjoyed a good spaghetti dinner, during which Madalyn smacked her lips and exclaimed, *"Molto buono!"* Very good.

"Why, Madalyn," I laughed, "you've been practicing."

After we did the dishes, we talked late into the night

and again our conversation turned to religion. She said she was reared a Presbyterian, but didn't explain what had made her turn away from the church.

"I have never seen any proof of God," she said, as she dried a platter. "But you're so sure, Rita. Why?"

"Well," I said, "I have never seen God either, Madalyn. But I have seen what He can do when you pray to Him."

Again we talked into the night. Finally, she sighed and stretched. "Rita, I love this house. There is something peaceful here."

"That is because Jesus is here, Madalyn," I answered quietly.

"Well," she said, looking around, "I can see His *pictures* everywhere."

"He's here, Madalyn. He is here. You don't see Him but He is here. Just like the wind. You don't see it, but you feel it."

As we talked, I became aware that there was Someone else in the room, Someone who was guiding my words. I knew that the last thing I wanted to do was to preach to Madalyn. Too many people have done this. She had told me about wild-eyed people who would come to her door day and night, thrusting tracts at her, pounding the Bible, and warning her of terrible calamities that would befall her if she did not immediately fall on her knees and repent. So this line of conversation was not what I had planned. However, I also had a deep-down assurance that what I was saying was what He wanted me to say.

Madalyn wondered why a God of love would allow His Son to die on the cross "in such a brutal way."

"He had to for us, Madalyn," I tried to explain. "Otherwise, you and I wouldn't be talking about Him now. Millions of Christians around the world wouldn't be living for Him.

"But it all comes down to this," I added. "If you love someone, you'll give your life for him. And that is what Jesus did for us."

I was silent for a moment, then I turned to her and said, "Madalyn, I would give my life for you if it were necessary."

"That's extreme," said Madalyn quietly.

"Well," I said, "that's what love is all about."

The next afternoon we went to the local college where we had been invited to debate. The auditorium was jammed with students. When we stepped out on stage, I introduced Madalyn as my friend. She replied that I was her friendly enemy.

As she spoke, explaining how she believed that there was no God, one could have heard a pin drop in the auditorium. I was grateful that no one screamed at her and called out obscenities as I had heard done elsewhere, even though some of the things she said grieved me. Then, I took the stand and gave my witness.

Again, neither of us pulled any punches. Madalyn and I like to debate openly, honestly. But through it all, the students could sense our sincerity for they seemed to follow every word, almost as if they were hanging onto the edges of their seats. I hoped that they got the message that there could be love and respect between people of opposite opinions.

That night after the debate as we drove home, Madalyn would not let me forget that Anita had asked for a Wayne Newton record. I had told Madalyn of how, a few years ago, Anita had seen the young singer on television, and had reacted as any typical teen-aged girl. Wayne Newton became her idol. At the time Anita couldn't walk because of recent operations, and the doctors said it might take years before she did. I read where Wayne Newton was due in Boston within a few months to do a New Year's show. I promised Anita that I would take her to see him.

"Mommie," she told me at the time, "I will walk for Christmas." Each day she strove but to no avail. On Christmas Day I had to push her to church in a wheelchair. I sat there grieving inside for Anita. She had wanted to walk so much. As we prayed, I asked

the Lord to give her the strength. It came time to receive Holy Communion, and I was kneeling in the
pew, my head down when Teresa took my arm. I
looked up and almost shouted in exultation. Anita had
risen from her wheelchair and had walked to the altar
rail to receive Communion. That was my Christmas
gift. When Wayne Newton arrived in Boston a few
days later, someone told him of Anita's interest in him,
and he invited us to his show as special guests. He dedicated his show to her and Anita was enraptured. From
that day on she improved dramatically.

Madalyn had listened intently as I told her this, and
now she made getting Anita the Wayne Newton record
her special project. She made us stop at three stores
until we found one, and insisted on buying it.

"Madalyn," I said, "you have God in your heart."

"Why?" she looked at me in surprise.

"Because God is love."

"Rita," she said, "you intrigue me."

The next morning I took Madalyn to the airport. We
were late, the highway was heavy with traffic, and she
was worried that we might not make it in time. It was
the only plane that she could catch that day, and she
had to make an appointment.

"Don't worry, Madalyn," I said. "God is with us."

She smiled wryly.

"Madalyn," I said, "you are an intelligent woman
and you should never say that there is no God for you
really don't know if there is one or not."

"Well, how can you be so sure?"

"Faith in God is a beautiful and special gift, and
with it one experiences security and joy," I said. "But
it isn't something that you have to strive for nor is it a
special award. You just have to accept it like knowing
the sun will rise tomorrow morning."

"Well," Madalyn said, quietly, "maybe next time I'll
say that I don't know if the sun will rise tomorrow
morning."

"Madalyn," I answered, "I believe He *does* exist just as I believe the sun *will* rise tomorrow morning. Oh, Madalyn," I added, "if everyone would accept Him, this world wouldn't be in such an awful mess. He is not a God of hatred and war, but is a loving, patient Father who, despite our mistakes, is always ready to forgive."

At this we drove up to the airport and Madalyn looked at her watch. "Hmmm," she exhaled gratefully, "I've still got ten minutes."

"See," I called out the window, as she walked to the door of the airport building, "He even gives you time when you need it."

She laughed, waved, and headed toward her boarding gate. I drove back to Brockton deep in thought. Why had God brought us two divergent people together? There must be some reason. Because of Madalyn, 1972 for me was quite a year.

What would 1973 be like? One thing I knew: It would be a year of decision—a year in which we would learn once and for all whether or not children could legally talk to their Father while attending public school in Massachusetts.

12.

Crash!

But before we saw much of 1973, I was again reminded how much I had to place my faith in the Lord rather than in my own understanding. We had been planning our usual Washington's Birthday-week trip to Washington to lobby for the national prayer amendment when the terrible accident happened.

It was the Saturday night before we were to leave on Sunday. Teresa and two girl friends had taken our old car and driven in to Boston to see Father McCormick, our old parish priest, who had become such a father to my girls. He was the one who had visited me in the hospital that day when I told him that I felt the Lord wanted me to try and get prayer back into the public school. We had kept in touch, and when we were at critical times with our prayer campaign—like the election, or when the bill was before the House—he'd always let me know he was praying for us.

That night the phone rang at 10 P.M. It was Father McCormick; he said that the girls had left and were on their way.

"Thank you, Father," I said, mentally noting that they would be home in about an hour. Anita was sleeping and I watched television for a while. Then I noticed it was 11:30 P.M. Still no Teresa. Oh, well, I figured, taking the other girls home may take a little longer. Midnight came. Then 1 A.M. Now I was frantic.

I started to dial the police but felt that at this time it was useless. What could I tell them? My daughter was out late? Now I began trembling violently. Fear clutched my heart and I collapsed on the sofa. *Oh, Teresa, my Teresa!* And then, like a gentle breeze from the sea that I remembered so well as a child, I felt His Presence. I turned to Him. "O Father," I prayed. "She may be dead, she may be alive. Only You know. But Father, right now, I release Teresa to You. She is Your child. Please take care of her."

I don't know how long I lay on that sofa, feeling the heaviness leave my soul. Then the phone rang. I lunged for it.

It was Teresa. "Oh, my baby, my baby!" I cried. "Are you all right?"

"Yes, Mom, don't worry . . . we had an accident but we're all all right."

"Are you sure, Honey?"

"Yes, Mom. Linda and Christina are okay too. Can you pick us up?"

I called Christina's sister, and she and I drove to the accident scene and picked them up. After Teresa came home, we sat at the kitchen table while she had some milk and told me what had happened.

She and the girls were on their way home when the car ran out of gas. They were on the expressway. But driving low on gas?

"Teresa," I interrupted, "how many times have I told you . . ."

"Now, Mom, don't interrupt."

"All right, Honey, go on . . ."

"Anyway, when the engine died we pulled over to the side and stopped in the breakdown lane. While we were wondering what to do, we suddenly saw in the mirror headlights of a car speeding right at us. He must have been doing 80 miles an hour!"

"Oh, no," I gasped.

"Mom, I screamed: 'My God, please help us!' The crash was as if we had exploded and our car shot way out onto the grass. For a while I didn't know what had happened. Then we all started talking and crying. And you know, Mom, not one of us was hurt. Even the kid driving the car that hit us was all right. He said he was confused, and apologized for hitting us."

Right there at the table I looked up and thanked Him.

But our trusty old car was a complete loss.

To me a car is vital—for my employment, whenever I can get it—and my work for God in lobbying for good legislation. Where I live, it is difficult to get around without a car, much less getting to Boston. But prospects for getting another car looked bleak.

First of all, my insurance company said they could pay me only a few hundred dollars for the loss of my car. I knew part of that had to be used for family expenses. I went to three different dealers. The answer was the same. "You just don't have the kind of credit it takes to get a car, Mrs. Warren." I could see what they meant. My working part-time here and there was no criterion for a good credit rating.

Again I put it all in the Lord's hands, and just stopped worrying. One day while riding with a friend, we passed a car agency. In my heart I felt that He wanted me to stop in there. I asked my friend to drive in. I asked to see what they had.

The dealer welcomed me, then looked at me quizzically for a moment and said: "Ma'm, we have a 1973 car here that should sell for four thousand dollars. It's a good car, but in order to move our inventory, we'll let it go for three thousand dollars. Somehow I felt you'd be interested in it."

He showed me the car. I fell in love with it. Nothing fancy, but a desert-tan Ford 2-door sedan which looked very dependable. It was one in which I felt I could take the girls around with full confidence.

But I had to shake my head. "It's beautiful," I said sadly, "and it's just the car I need, but I'm afraid I don't have the credit for it."

"Well," he said, thinking I suppose, that I was trying to get him to come down more on his price, "I wish we could shave something off the price, but this is rock-bottom for us. Why don't you think it over?" And then he added with a wink (knowing my school battle) ". . . and say a prayer."

I left, feeling that it was useless for me to even think about it. But when I got home Teresa said that the insurance man had called. I dialed his number. "Mrs. Warren," boomed a jovial voice, "I've got good news for you. An assessment has been made of your loss, and you'll be getting a check in the mail for fifteen hundred dollars."

It had something to do with the other driver's liability. I couldn't quite understand it but felt it best to just say, "Fine!" and ask no more questions.

Fifteen hundred dollars! I did some quick figuring. That would let me pay off my debts and still have a thousand dollars to put down on the car. In ten minutes I was back at the dealer. I was very frank about my credit prospects.

He thought for a bit, then said: "Well, normally, one thousand dollars should be a very acceptable down payment on a three-thousand-dollar car. Let's put it through, and see what happens."

For the next two days I prayed: "Lord, You know I need a car to do Your work. And You know what kind of car it should be. I have a feeling that it is this tan one. But no matter, I will leave it up to You."

On the morning of the third day the dealer called me. "Mrs. Warren," he said, "your credit came through. When can you come in and pick up your car?"

Yes, the One whose eye is on the sparrow, even arranges transportation!

He also made sure Massachusetts children could sing Christmas carols in their schools again in 1973.

In March, the bill that Representatives Mary Fantasia and Raymond Flynn and I filed to override the Board of Education's Christmas guidelines came up for legislation.

It was approved by both the House of Representatives and Senate and went before Governor Sargent for his signature. He signed it into law at 11 A.M. on Good Friday, April 20, 1973. Representatives Mary Fantasia and Raymond Flynn, plus about a dozen concerned parents, and I stood beside his desk as he signed the bill which empowered local school committees to determine to what extent their local schools should observe religious holidays.

As Governor Sargent wrote his signature on the bill, he said that he believed it important "that schools have a right to determine exactly how they wish to celebrate a religious event."

As he signed the bill and newspaper photographers flashed their lights, I wondered how soon it would be before the same thing took place with our school-prayer bill.

We did not have to wait long to find out.

I got word from the Clerk of the House of Representatives that our prayer bill would be up before the House shortly.

Would it be the culmination of all the battles that hundreds of people and I had fought the past four years? I knew that all our hopes and dreams had been put in this one bill.

In a few days we would know—one way or another.

13.

A Minute in History

Summer, 1973. I'll never forget awakening that morning. A hot, early sun was already flooding my bedroom, and I lay in bed for a moment, aware that this was a special day—but in my half-awake state not exactly sure why. Then the realization struck me, and I raised my hands in exultation.

Today the prayer bill would be heard and debated in the House of Representatives!

Before one o'clock in the afternoon, our good friend Marilyn Layton, Teresa, Anita, and I were climbing the State House steps. I looked up at the statue of General Hooker and winked. I was feeling pretty good. As we headed toward the gallery, one of the Representatives, who was against the prayer bill, waved at me.

"Hi, Mike," I called. "I presume you have changed your mind?"

He stopped, grinned, and scratched the back of his head. "Rita," he sighed, "when are you going to give up? It's not going to pass. We will all just go through the motions and just like last time, it will hit that old constitutional snag and *phftt* . . . it will all be over."

"Mike," I answered, looking him straight in the eye. "Don't underestimate the power of God." He gave a quick laugh, shrugged, and headed into the meeting chamber.

As the others and I settled in the gallery, the Representatives slowly filed in. They were talking with each other, shuffling papers on their desks, getting ready for a busy afternoon. I wanted to shout, "Hurry! Hurry! There is important work to be done today!"

As we watched, bill after bill came before the House. The discussions droned on and votes were taken. We became more and more anxious. Finally, late in the afternoon the Clerk of the House stood up and announced *the* bill.

"Bill Number 4890," he called, "an act allowing for meditation and prayer in the public schools."

The floor of the House became a hubbub as representatives rose to their feet, some to speak for the bill, others to speak against it. The main contention seemed to be the word *prayer*.

"But that is unconstitutional!" was the rallying cry of those opposing it. I could do nothing but sit with my head bowed, praying.

Finally I could sense that it was nearing the time for a vote on the bill. I looked around at the gallery. Outside of our tiny group, it was completely empty. "Dear God," I prayed, "wouldn't it be wonderful if some children could come in here now as a witness for You."

The Clerk of the House stood to call the vote. At that instant, the gallery doors behind us burst open and a deluge of children poured down the steps to occupy most of the seats.

I sat transfixed. The bustle of the children caught the attention of the men on the floor, and everyone looked up.

The vote was called.

I sat there, holding my breath.

The red and green lights began flashing on . . . green, red, green, green, green. I lost count. But when the voting was complete, it was easy to see on the boards. Green had won. The final vote was 170 in favor, 50 against.

For several minutes our little group sat in the gallery quietly giving thanks. Then, our knees still weak from the excitement, we walked downstairs into the corridor.

The Representative with whom I talked before the session tried to slip by us. He turned his head. I couldn't resist hailing him. "That's all right, Mike. Nobody will hold it against you."

A Representative hurried up to me. "Rita," he said, "where did you get all those children?"

"Mr. Piro," I said, "I didn't bring them in here, God did."

As it turned out, they were a group of school children from the northern part of the state who were touring Boston. This happened to be the moment when they were brought into the State House to see a meeting in session!

But I still believe God arranged the timing.

That night I could hardly sleep.

The next day we sat in the visitors' gallery of the Senate Chamber. This time the debate seemed to center around the fact that the bill made the minute of meditation and prayer mandatory. Again, the opponents pointed to the Constitution. They used the same argument that had been used to knock down every prayer amendment that had been brought up before Congress in Washington. My hands gripped the gallery rail till my knuckles whitened.

And then one Senator came up with a recommendation. He recommended that the wording of the bill be changed slightly—by just one word, in fact. Where the bill said, "One minute in duration shall be observed for meditation and prayer," he recommended that it read: ". . . for meditation *or* prayer."

That one word did it! Now even an Atheist could take part in this minute with a clear conscience; if he wanted to meditate about an upcoming biology test, that was up to him. But it was still an official recognition that prayer was allowed. A definite time would be set aside for it.

I thought back a few years ago to the time at our kitchen table when Teresa said, "Even if they just gave us a minute, we could all sit together and pray silently, each kid praying in the way he wants. If someone didn't want to pray, they could just think about their homework or something, and wouldn't have to feel funny about it." It was a real prophecy.

After the word change, there was little more debate on the bill. The main reason for this, I feel, was the referendum. As one Senator said, "The people have already spoken for this bill; let it pass."

The vote was 27 in favor of the bill, 8 against. I sank back in my seat, breathing thanks to Him who really made it all possible. It was all over—all over now except for the formality of the bill going back to the House for a reading, and then to the Governor for his signature.

It went to Governor Sargent for this on July 25. While we waited through the days for him to sign, I caught up on some housework, took Anita to the doctor for a check-up, and had a picnic for the children who had been doing a lot of legwork for the prayer bill. I wasn't really counting the days that it had been sitting on the Governor's desk. I knew he had ten days in which to sign it. If he took all ten to do it, it was all right with me.

It was my friend Marilyn, who told me.

I was getting dinner on the table when she called.

"Rita?" her voice sounded strange. "Did you see the news on TV?"

"No," I said, holding a stirring spoon in midair.

"He vetoed it."

The spoon dropped from my hand.

"But, *why?*" I gasped.

"The same old thing," she said. "The Attorney General said that the bill would violate the Constitution."

I couldn't say anything more. The boulder that we had rolled to the top of the hill had fallen back on us again. I weakly thanked Marilyn for calling, hung up the phone, and sat staring at the wall. The next thing I remember was Anita tugging at my arm. The sauce I was preparing had boiled over.

Later that evening I read the story in the newspaper. Governor Sargent admitted that the prayer proposal was "easily understandable and is certainly well intentioned" but that "in good conscience" he could not approve the legislation. Approval, he said, would only serve to prolong a continuing controversy and would "once again require judicial resolution."

By the time I finished reading his statement, I became so angry that I slapped the paper down on the table, frightening Anita and Teresa.

"Mama, what's wrong?" asked Teresa.

"The Governor and the Attorney General are wrong," I snapped. "And we are going to inform them of it."

I got on the phone and called the folks in our group. I told them I felt there was only one thing to do: for as many of us as possible to go down to the State House tomorrow and face the Attorney General on the prayer bill.

Early next morning I was on the phone with his secretary. "Yes," she said. "The Attorney General can see you at two o'clock in the afternoon."

"Fine!" I said, "we'll be there."

The afternoon was gray and threatening, matching the mood of our little group of ten as we met outside the State House. Together we entered the building and marched into the Attorney General's office.

We faced him over his desk. The Attorney General of Massachusetts was a distinguished-looking handsome man in his early thirties. In a smooth, calm voice he welcomed us, and invited us to sit down. At any other time I think I would have enjoyed talking with him.

But now my temper was dangerously boiling, and I couldn't sit. I stood there looking at him, fire in my eyes. And then God's words came to me again: "Remember, Rita. It's My battle, not yours."

I let out a deep breath, praying for strength to say the right thing, to not lose my temper. For now I knew for certain that if I did I would accomplish nothing but be written off as a crackpot or troublemaker.

I drew in a breath. "Sir, I respect your position as Attorney General of the state of Massachusetts, and I respect your judgment. But, sir, it is only your opinion that the prayer bill is unconstitutional."

He continued looking at me, smiling, and he seemed awfully glad to have an answer for me. His answer was that there was a possibility that the Governor's veto might be overridden. In fact, he said, it was being discussed right then on the floor of the House of Representatives. Why didn't we go over there? he suggested.

I didn't know whether to kiss him or shake his hand. In seconds, our little group was on its way to the House of Representatives. There had been a recess after the discussion, and now the men were filing back into the House to vote.

Marilyn Layton and I didn't think we could stand watching the voting board. We stationed ourselves on each side of the door leading into the House. "Pray!" I whispered to her. She looked at me and nodded.

After the Representatives filed in, the door was closed. Marilyn and I just stood there, our heads bowed, praying that God's will would be done inside that chamber.

Suddenly, we could hear an explosion of shouts filling the air inside the room behind the door. "Yippee! Hurrah!"

The door flew open, and a Representative dashed out and began clapping me on the back. "Mrs. Warren!" he cried, "You've done it again!"

We looked inside the room. A beautiful predominance of green lights filled the voting board. The vote was 171 to 50 to override the veto.

"Oh, thank You, Father," I sighed, as I slumped against the door. Jubilation filled the room with men and women Representatives laughing and talking. Representative Vincent Piro rushed over and hugged me. "Mrs. Warren," he cried, his eyes brimming with tears. "God bless you! God bless you!"

Tears were streaming down my cheeks. "God bless *you!*" I cried. "God bless all of you who voted for prayer!"

The next day our group sat in the gallery of the Senate. We sat there most of the afternoon waiting for the bill to be brought up, and there was still no word of it. Senator Walter Boverini came up the stairs and stepped over to us. "Mrs. Warren," he said, "why don't you go home. I'm sure the veto will be overridden here, too."

I looked up at him in surprise. "Oh, no," I exclaimed. "We have a responsibility." All of us sitting there, I'm sure, felt like expectant mothers. When the big event happened, we had to be there.

Finally, at 4:30 P.M., the question of overriding the veto came up for discussion. I remember that Senator Robert A. Hall from Lunenburg stated something to the effect that "a moment of voluntary meditation or prayer is a long way from the establishment of state religion."

There was a lot of discussion, and then suddenly a number of Senators rose to their feet. I wasn't sure of what was taking place; by now I think I was in somewhat of a daze so much had happened these past few days. Suddenly, Senator Boverini came bounding up the stairs, his face beaming. "Mrs. Warren," he said, "you all can go home now. The veto has been overridden!" The vote was 27–8.

"God bless you, Senator Boverini!" I cried. All of us rushed downstairs to shake hands with the Senators who had voted to override the veto. In our exuberance, I am sure we also shook hands with some of the men who voted to let it stand.

I phoned Mary Fantasia that evening. "Mary," I asked, "will the Governor have to sign the bill now?"

She explained that now there was no need for him to sign the bill. The very act of overriding his veto sufficed. In ninety days, according to the statute of Massachusetts, the bill would officially become the law of the land in our state.

I circled the date on my calendar. There was one place that I had to be on October 23, 1973. And that was in a classroom of our public school in Brockton. I wanted to see for myself children being given the opportunity to pray.

The circled date on my calendar came closer and closer. On August 6, 1973, in anticipation of the day, Joseph F. Plouffe, Assistant Superintendent of the Brockton Public Schools, sent a memo to all Brockton school principals. The first paragraph read:

> Chapter 71, Section 1A, of the General Laws of the Commonwealth of Massachusetts has been amended to have at the commencement of the first class each day a period not to exceed one minute of silence for meditation or prayer.

The balance of the memo explained it further in detail.

Tuesday, October 23, 1973, would be the first day it would be instituted.

Of course I *had* to be there.

I chose Ashfield Elementary School which was near my home. The morning of October 23 dawned gray and foggy. But as I drove to the school there seemed to be a brightness to the day that no earthly fog or gloom could obliterate.

My heart quickened as I reached the school. The

parking lot was alive with television crews and newspaper photographers, since our Brockton public schools were the first to comply with the new Massachusetts law.

I got out of my car, walked to the front entrance of the school. As I stepped through the door, I suddenly realized that I was entering a school not to plead or complain, but to celebrate.

As I walked down the hallway, my heels clicking in rhythm with the beating of my heart, I was caught up in the intensity of the moment. I thought back to that other October in 1969. Four years had gone by since that fateful afternoon when Teresa came home and told me they couldn't pray in school.

I chose to visit the fourth-grade classroom. I'm not sure why. Perhaps it was because the children were nine and ten years old, old enough to appreciate what they were now allowed to do, but still virtually untouched by a blasé world. Would they be the beginning of a new generation of students to whom God would be as much a natural part of classroom life as writing a composition and following the voyages of Columbus?

I climbed steps already worn by thousands of little feet, and then walked down the hall to the fourth-grade room. I hesitated at the door for an instant, then took a deep breath, opened the door and walked in.

Twenty-seven little boys and girls twisted and fidgeted in their seats, as they waited for class to begin. I smiled at Miss Del Surdo, the teacher. She nodded back, and I sat down at one side of the room.

The starting bell rang, the rustling at the desks stopped, and Miss Del Surdo stepped to the front of the class.

"Children," she said, "today we are going to do something different, something which we will be doing from now on. After we say the pledge of allegiance, we will pause for a minute of meditation or prayer."

The teacher then walked to the back of the classroom and stood there. I wondered what would happen. I understood that no child had been coached or primed on what was to come.

And then, one of the most controversial minutes in history began taking place. I leaned forward in my seat. There was a hush in the classroom as if all eternity poised to listen. One could even hear the slight patter of rain at the window.

That was all she said: "We will pause for a minute of meditation or prayer."

As the teacher's words died away, twenty-seven little voices rose in unison as they recited the pledge of allegiance. And then, each child, without any self-consciousness or sideways glance, folded his hands before him, bowed his little head and—in my heart I knew—communicated with the One who said: "Suffer the little children and let them come unto Me" (*see* Matthew 19:14).

My breath caught, tears streamed down my face, and my heart cried out in gratitude.

"O Father," I sighed, "You said that a little child would lead them. May these little children lead all of us, who have mistakenly placed our trust in the world and in man's thinking. May these little children lead us into placing our complete faith in You, so that Your Holy Spirit may reign supreme in our hearts evermore, guiding us, inspiring us, giving us new life and freedom through Your Son, Jesus Christ."

Prayer had come back to the public schools in Massachusetts.

Epilogue

But only part of the battle has been won. I do not feel that I can rest until every child in every state has the same opportunity to communicate with his Maker as do the children of Massachusetts.

Today I see our nation filled with anxiety. Within the past decade we have seen an onslaught of materialism and immorality surge across our land. We have seen the powers of darkness in the growing crime, proliferating pornography, and laxness of moral standards in business and public office.

There is an answer to this slide—one given us thousands of years ago. As the Lord told Solomon then, He tells us today: "If my people who are called by my name humble themselves, and pray and seek my face, and turn from their wicked ways, then will I hear from heaven, and will forgive their sin and heal their land" (2 Chronicles 7:14 RSV).

I pray that all of us will heed that answer. May we always be able to humble ourselves, and seek His face freely in our homes, churches, and schools.

To this end I shall continue working with all who are endeavoring to get the new amendment to the U.S. Constitution passed to make this possible. It should be an amendment that will guarantee both freedom of religion—freedom from government control and freedom of religious expression.

A number of persons and groups are sponsoring

amendments before the United States Congress to return voluntary prayer to schools. All of us should write our U.S. Representatives and Senators, urging them to vote for the amendments.

I also believe a bill like the Massachusetts prayer bill can be passed in every state. Many people have written me that they will try to get such a bill passed in their own state. I pray that everyone will work through his own state legislator to achieve this goal. And then the bells will ring not only at Saint Coleman's as Father McCormick promised they would, but all over the nation.

To find the names and current mailing addresses of your national and state Representatives, simply phone your board of election, which is usually listed under the name of your county in the local phone directory. You can usually also get this information by calling your local newspaper. Remember that a personal letter is most effective; petitions, printed cards, and mimeographed letters are not as influential.

It is my feeling that the type of prayer law we now have in Massachusetts can be acceptable in any state— completely voluntary, since it offers prayer *or* meditation. It imposes nothing on anyone and is not discriminatory. Yet, it affords those who wish to pray a recognized opportunity to do so. If one does not pray, he need not feel set apart but can, as Teresa said early in our campaign, meditate on his homework or plans for the day. In either event, I cannot see where this quiet minute for prayer or meditation cannot help but benefit everyone.

As the battle continues, I know that I am not fighting alone. I have learned to use the word *us*. I think of the thousands of people throughout our country who have long been involved in the school-prayer campaign: government leaders, business people, and men and women from all walks of life. I think of the fine and dedicated lawyers who have helped me in the struggle. I think of our little group of workers—the housewives, their husbands, the grandmothers and grandfathers, and all the children.

I think of Teresa whose school experience started it all. She graduated from high school in 1974, and is now a grown woman, and meeting the responsibilities of adulthood.

Still with me is dear, patient Anita, who almost always accompanies me wherever I go. I thank God for every day He gives us together.

My son, Bobby, is married, has a son, and is studying to be a minister.

And I thank God for Louis Angelo, the young man who helped us so much. A graduate of Boston State College, he is now a teacher in the Brockton public schools, where he sees the fruit of his labor when he daily tells his students they have a minute for meditation or prayer.

And always in my prayers is Madalyn Murray O'Hair. We still treasure our friendship, and I feel we always will. And even though we will fight toe to toe on behalf of our individual beliefs, we will do it in love, respecting each other's right to her own philosophy. I in no way wish to convey the impression that I have converted or intend to convert Madalyn, or that anyone else can convert her. For only God has the power to reach the heart of man. Of course, I hold in my heart that someday she will have the rich security of a faith in a loving God.

I hope that I have also grown. In my battles I have argued with many people. I will have to admit to having a quick temper, which I am now better able to control. And for that I thank God. For as I have learned, a temper accomplishes nothing. It is the Lord's battle, not ours.

What battles I face in the future, only God knows. All I know is that they will continue, and He will give me the strength to fight them. When people called to congratulate me about the school-prayer bill, I told them a lot of people should be congratulated. Besides, it wasn't I who did anything, it was Jesus. Me? I'm a nobody. But I have learned that a nobody—with God—can move mountains.

SINCE THEN . . .

. . . more exciting battles.

By mid-1976, at least 15 states had passed laws similar to the Massachusetts statute calling for one minute of silence in the classroom for meditation or prayer. And many more states are considering such a statute. Each time I saw news of another state passing this law, I thanked God. It was beginning to happen just as I hoped. Individuals who believed in freedom to pray had worked through their state's legislature.

But trouble brewed on the horizon.

I had no idea of this, however, as I found myself being called on more and more to speak before civic groups, churches, college students, and even before legislatures of other states such as Ohio which is now considering this law. When I spoke before the Ohio Legislature, I was suddenly impelled to conclude my speech by telling them my motto "With God all things are possible." There was a standing ovation and only later did I learn that the Ohio House of Representatives' motto also is: "With God all things are possible."

Yet, all the time good things were happening elsewhere, I was disturbed that this law was not being fully implemented in my own state's schools. The reason for this was that some of the Massachusetts schools had officials who questioned the law's constitutionality. Thus, some schools were observing the silent minute, others were not.

But God works in mysterious ways.

For as I was continuing to speak out in various Massachusetts cities for the implementation of this law, the opposition was marshaling its forces to wipe this law off the books in our state.

In February 1976 it took its opportunity.

The school committee of Framingham, a city in eastern Massachusetts, had just implemented this law in its public schools.

Immediately, the Civil Liberties Union of Massachusetts filed suit challenging this law on behalf of 12 local pupils and their parents.

Framingham's town counsel expressed his opinion that the prayer statute was unconstitutional and thus he wouldn't defend the school committee.

At this, the chairman of the school committee turned to a local Framingham attorney, Alfred Mainini, and asked him to represent the committee at the court hearing of the Civil Liberties Union's request for a preliminary injunction restraining the committee from implementing the prayer statute.

He accepted the case even though he had only two days to prepare. His arguments against the injunction were accepted by District Court Judge Walter J. Skinner who denied the Civil Liberties Union's preliminary request, and then granted a request to convene a panel of three U.S. District judges who would decide on the constitutionality of the statute.

Their verdict would be a landmark decision with far-reaching consequences. If the U.S. judges decided against the law, this would have repercussions in all other states who had the law or were considering it. Years of struggle by many people would be wasted. And teachers would again have to be careful about mentioning prayer in schools. This is the intimidating effect such an adverse ruling would have.

I got on my knees and prayed that the Lord's will would be done, that God, through our Lord Jesus Christ would guide the hearts and minds of the judges and everyone involved in this case.

Then, I got into my car and drove to Framingham.

There I met Alfred Mainini. In my heart I knew that he had been called on by the Lord to defend this law. I was grateful to him for taking this stand to defend what I felt were the rights of the majority. But one man, alone, I thought, fighting against such opposition?

Then I realized that he was not alone. For he was standing on the side of God. And I knew that many people were praying for him and Framingham.

I offered to help him in any way I could. For I knew that the school committee did not have any money to pay him for his services.

He said: "Never mind; as the father of three children, I feel that I must represent the majority of people who want their children to have the freedom to pray as they wish."

During the trial, the spokesman for the American Civil Liberties Union argued that: "daily, mandatory observance of a period of silence for prayer or meditation is a coercive program which should have no place in the life of public school." He claimed that the law illegally infringed on parents' rights to direct the religious training of their children.

Attorney Mainini replied that: "This law does not mandate prayer; it orders a moment of silence to be utilized by the student for any purpose including prayer."

The trial took a long time and then the three judges went into deliberation. They were: Chief Circuit Court Judge Frank M. Coffin, District Court Judges Frank J. Murray and Walter J. Skinner. They were in deliberation for four months.

On Thursday, September 2nd, 1976, they rendered their decision. I will never forget when I heard the verdict. I was standing at my kitchen sink doing the dishes when the telephone rang. It was Jean Cole, reporter with the Boston *Herald American*, telling me the good news.

I was so happy I danced through the house praising the Lord.

The next morning as I unrolled the newspaper, there were the headlines:

U.S. Court Approves Meditation, Prayer for Mass. Schools

'MINUTE OF SILENCE' LAW UPHELD

Here are some excerpts from the newspaper story:

In a long awaited and historic decision, a three-judge federal district court yesterday declared constitutional the Massachusetts law ordering a minute of silence for the purpose of meditation or prayer in all public schools.

The unanimous ruling will have repercussions in all communities that have not obeyed the legislative mandate. The decision could eventually have national impact if it is upheld in a U.S. Supreme Court appeal.

The judges found no rights of children or their parents violated by the state statute. They said it is inherently "neutral" as was no other contested prayer law in the country.

"If a student's beliefs preclude prayer in the setting of a minute of silence in a schoolroom, he may turn his mind silently toward a secular topic or simply remain silent," the judges said.

. . . in appraising the amended statute, [the judges] said they were mindful that government's attitude toward religion must be one of "wholesome neutrality."

". . . Thus the effect of the [law] is to accommodate students who desire to use the minute of silence for prayer or religious meditation, and also

other students who prefer to reflect upon secular
matters.

". . . The statute and guidelines do not have a
primary effect of favoring or sponsoring religion,"
they found.

This was it, I thought, as I held the newspaper before
me: the law must not promote religion, nor must it
negate it. I remembered that Judge Murray said that the
First Amendment should be read with the understanding that the United States is a country whose "heritage
is religious and whose people in large measure adhere
to a variety of religious beliefs. The requirements of the
First Amendment do not implicate hostility to religion
or indifference toward religious groups; they do not
impart a preference for those who believe in no religion
or demand primary devotion to the secular."

I also thought of another famous case referred to by
the judges in their decision (Yoder vs. Wisconsin) in
which the court stated: "The history and culture of
Western civilization reflect a strong tradition of parental concern for the nature and upbringing of their children. This primary role of the parents in the rearing of
their children is now established beyond debate as an
enduring American tradition."

The Framingham decision had a wide effect in the
state. The Massachusetts attorney general, Francis X.
Bellotti, now requested the state's commissioner of
education, who earlier was of the opinion that the law
was unconstitutional, to order its implementation state-
wide.

In addition, the American Civil Liberties Union of
Massachusetts decided not to appeal to the U.S. Supreme Court.

Meanwhile, during the long court trial, I had become
increasingly concerned with how opposing groups
seemed to find it so easy to step in time and again to
effectively negate prayer laws throughout the country.

For this reason on May 28, 1976, with the help of God and Attorney Alfred Mainini, we formed the Christian Civil Liberties Union, Inc. Our purpose is: "An educational nondenominational organization to protect the Constitutional rights of the people of the United States, to support a moment of silence for meditation or prayer in the public schools. To do any and all things necessary to improve the educational system in the public schools of the United States."

We are so grateful to Attorney Mainini for his help on this. Nine parents have joined me on the Board of Directors, and the Christian Civil Liberties Union is growing with members joining from all over the United States. Our address is 898 Court Street, Brockton, Massachusetts 02402.

Starting this organization was the best birthday gift we could give to our country on its bicentennial. We hope and pray that soon the bells of churches throughout America will peal in celebration of the fact that school children in all fifty states will have the opportunity of this silent minute for prayer.

I pray also that our nation will be led by our Lord, through His Son Jesus Christ. For only through Him will we reach the fullness of our destiny.

Key-Word Books for Further Reading

Appointment in Jerusalem by Lydia and Derek Prince. Now told for the first time in paperback! The amazing story of a young woman's walk in the spirit. Lydia was a school teacher who dared to be led by the Holy Spirit into the city where God had hidden the key to the Future. #4109-1.

The Morning Star: God's Gift for Daily Living by Denise Rinker Adler. A collection of helpful devotional thoughts for the woman who is "bounded on the north by a kitchen sink, on the east by an ironing board, on the west by the children, and the south by the washing machine." The author discovers in the lives of Enoch, Sarah, Moses, Gideon, and a host of other biblical characters, inspiration which speaks to everyday needs. #91007.

Tracks of a Fellow Struggler by John R. Claypool. For almost two decades as a pastor, John Claypool participated in the drama of suffering and death—but it was always happening to someone else. But now his own eight-year-old daughter, Laura Lee, was diagnosed as having acute leukemia. John Claypool's personal struggle will help you learn to handle grief in your own life. #91008.

The Liberty of Obedience by Elisabeth Elliot. After the death of her husband by the Auca Indians she spent two years in Ecuador to study this strange people. Living in a culture whose values differed so sharply forced her to reevaluate her Christian faith. #91018.

A Slow and Certain Light by Elisabeth Elliot. Do you really know what God's will is for you and your life? How does your own self-will fit into this master plan? A collection of observations from Elisabeth Elliot's personal experience and from the Bible on why and how God does, in fact, guide His children. #91009.

New Man . . . New World by Leighton Ford. Reaffirms the age-old truth that new men in Christ inevitably create new worlds. This book offers an authentic pattern for life which substitutes faith, hope, excitement—life in Christ—for alienation, confusion, and meaninglessness. #91013.

Parables for Parents and Other Original Sinners by Tom Mullen. 30 rib-tickling reflections on the realities of parenthood. There's a lot of wisdom mixed in with the wit of these delightful "parables" based on the antics and attitudes of the author's own children. #4100-8.

Birthdays, Holidays and Other Disasters by Tom Mullen. A look at the little things that make up our daily lives. Delightful, hilarious and very Christian perspectives that give the reader an insightful experience into happy Christian living. #4105-9.

Happiness Is Still Homemade by T. Cecil Myers. How to turn "daylight and dishes" into "moonlight and roses"—all marriage long. Here are tested principles for a happy home life for anyone interested in making marriage more fulfilling and the home more Christian and creative. #91019.

Living on Tiptoe by T. Cecil Myers. Shows you how by prayer and faith you can improve your own emotional health. Discover how to worry correctly, how to love yourself in the right way, and how to accept positively what cannot be changed. #4104-0.

Conversational Prayer by Rosalind Rinker. Drops the traditional patterns for prayer and adopts the open language of the heart: honesty, love, simplicity. Provides specific help in learning and teaching how to pray. #91003.

I Stand by the Door by Helen Smith Shoemaker. University undergraduates, factory workers, young married couples—all these were, to Sam Shoemaker, special and individual people for whom he poured out all his many talents. Helen Shoemaker's vivid portrait of her husband's life. #4102-4.

The Secret of Effective Prayer by Helen Smith Shoemaker. Here is a book which continually affirms the reality of answered prayer. But it does more than that: the author shares with us the "secrets" of praying that she has discovered in her efforts to know God's will. #91004.